9-11

TIVE?

9-11

WAS THERE AN ALTERNATIVE?

NOAM CHOMSKY

AN OPEN MEDIA BOOK

7

SEVEN STORIES PRESS
NEW YORK

The Open Media Series is edited by Greg Ruggiero and archived by the Tamiment Collection at New York University.

Front cover photo by Greg Ruggiero: September 11, 2001, view from Canal Street and Hudson.

Back cover photo, Official White House photograph by Pete Souza: President Barack Obama and Vice President Joe Biden, along with members of the national security team, monitor the mission against Osama bin Laden in the Situation Room of the White House, May 1, 2001. Seated, from left, are: Brigadier General Marshall B. "Brad" Webb, Assistant Commanding General, Joint Special Operations Command; Deputy National Security Advisor Denis McDonough; Secretary of State Hillary Rodham Clinton; and Secretary of Defense Robert Gates. Standing, from left, are: Admiral Mike Mullen, Chairman of the Joint Chiefs of Staff; National Security Advisor Tom Donilon; Chief of Staff Bill Daley; Tony Binken, National Security Advisor to the Vice President; Audrey Tomason Director for Counterterrorism; John Brennan, Assistant to the President for Homeland Security and Counterterrorism; and Director of National Intelligence James Clapper. Please note: a classified document seen in this photograph has been obscured.

Book design by Jon Gilbert

Library of Congress Cataloging-in-Publication Data

Chomsky, Noam.
 9-11 : updated and expanded after the assassination of Osama Bin Laden, with a new introduction, Was there an alternative? / Noam Chomsky
   p. cm. -- (An open media book)
 ISBN 978-1-60980-343-8 (pbk.)
 1. September 11 Terrorist Attacks, 2001. 2. Terrorism--Prevention. I. Title. II. Title: Nine-eleven.
 HV6432.7.C48 2011
 973.931--dc23

                                    2011027901

9 8 7 6 5 4 3 2 1

Printed in the USA.

I would like to thank David Peterson and Shifra Stern for invaluable assistance with current media research particularly.

—NOAM CHOMSKY

Contents

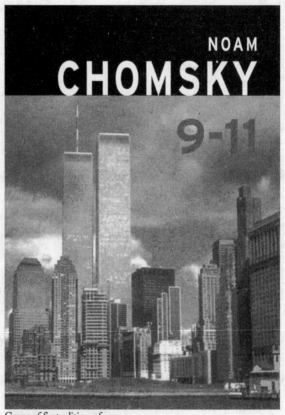

Cover of first edition of *9-11*.

EDITOR'S NOTE

The book you are holding was conceived, produced, and published as an act of protest. From the weeks immediately following the attacks in Washington and New York in 2001, to those immediately following the US assassination of Osama bin Laden in Pakistan in 2011, Noam Chomsky has highlighted the lessons of history and advocated adhering to the basic tenets of human rights as the best ways to break step from the drum beats for war. In opposing violence as a political solution, Chomsky's analysis of policy and media coverage in the United States poses difficult questions. Should the US obey the International Court? Should the US obey UN resolutions? Should the US abide by the same principles and rules to which it holds other countries? What have the US wars since 9/11 accomplished? The facts are harsh: Thousands of US soldiers have been killed on foreign soil. Untold numbers of people in Afghanistan, Pakistan, and Iraq have been killed, injured, displaced, or detained. What are the consequences? Is the world a better place? Was there an alternative?

Was there an alternative? This is now one of the great moral and political questions of our time, and it is the title of Chomsky's new essay written to introduce this third edition *9-11*. Written in June 2011, Chomsky's text examines the impact and consequences of US foreign policy up to the assassination of Osama bin Laden in Abbottabad, Pakistan, and reflects on what may have resulted if the crimes against humanity committed on 9/11 had been "approached as a crime, with an international operation to apprehend the likely suspects."

In exploring possible answers, Chomsky reviews another notorious September 11 and major historical events, many of which are simply overlooked and forgotten in the United States. In discussing the operation against bin Laden, he also touches on the "imperial mentality" and the decision to name the mission "Operation Geronimo." "The casual choice of the name," writes Chomsky, "is reminiscent of the ease with which we name our murder weapons after victims of our crimes: Apache, Blackhawk, Tomahawk. . . . We might react differently if the Luftwaffe were to call its fighter planes 'Jew' and 'Gypsy.'"

For many who read Chomsky for the first time, his analysis can be disorienting because he focuses precisely on those facts that have been systemically under-reported or completely ignored by mainstream media. Consequences of US actions in Nicaragua, for example, are not widely known or remembered in the United States. As Chomsky said in an e-mail while we were working on the book, "These facts have been completely removed from history. One has to practically scream them from the rooftops."

Ten years after its original publication, the overlooked facts and difficult questions Chomsky poses in *9-11* continue to be heard over the rooftops of official history. Despite wars, despite indefinite detentions, despite drones and increasing militarization, people in this country and around the world have shown their resistance not just in the streets, but also by what we read.

A "Surprise Best Seller"—to quote the title of an article about it in the *New York Times*[1]—*9-11* has been published in more than two dozen countries and has appeared on multiple bestseller lists, including the *Washington Post*, the *Los Angeles Time*s, the *Boston Globe*, and the *New York Times*. An article about it in *The New Yorker* stated, "*9-11* was practically the only counter-narrative out there at a time when questions tended to be drowned out by a chorus, led by the entire United States Congress, of 'God Bless America.'" It was one of the few places where the other side of the case could be found."[2]

Published years before Facebook and Twitter were invented, people found out about the book largely through community bookstores, word of mouth, newspapers, public radio, and even CNN, where Chomsky debated the book as a guest on *American Morning* with Paula Zahn.[3]

Bookstores, particularly independents like St. Mark's Bookshop and City Lights, became a driving force of distribution and sales. "Seeking to explain the book's success," wrote Michael Massing in the *New York Times*, "booksellers cite its succinct title, striking cover (a stark black-and-white picture of the twin towers before the attacks), low price . . . and accessible question-and-answer format. 'People are coming in every day, asking, "What can I read that can give me some understanding of what's happening?'" said Virginia Harabin, the floor manager at the Politics and Prose Bookstore in Washington. 'This is the one I recommend.'"[4]

"The primary challenge facing the people of the world is, literally, survival," writes Chomsky.[5] If we indeed survive our government's propensity for confrontation and violence over diplomacy, it may be because we break away from the news feed long enough to heed dissident voices like Chomsky's, published in pamphlets, posted online, spoken at protests, and shouted from the rooftops.

Greg Ruggiero
July 12, 2011
Union County, New Jersey

NOTES

1. Michael Massing, "Surprise Best Seller Blames U.S.," *New York Times*, May 2, 2002, B11.
2. Louis Menand, "Faith, Hope, and Clarity: September 11th and the American Soul," *The New Yorker*, September 16, 2002.
3. *American Morning* with Paula Zahn, live debate with Noam Chomsky, May 30, 2002, transcript posted here: http://www.cnn.com/TRANSCRIPTS/0205/30/ltm.01.html.
4. Michael Massing, "Surprise Best Seller Blames U.S.," *New York Times*, May 2, 2002, B11.
5. Noam Chomsky, "Delaying Doomsday: This Century's Challenges," April 24, 2008, distributed by the New York Times Syndicate and forthcoming in Noam Chomsky, *Making the Future: The Unipolar Imperial Moment*, City Lights Books/Open Media Series.

Was There an Alternative?

As I write (mid-June 2011), we are approaching the tenth anniversary of the horrendous atrocities of September 11, 2001, which, it is commonly held, changed the world. A few weeks ago, on May 1, the presumed mastermind of the crime, Osama bin Laden, was assassinated in Pakistan by a team of elite US commandos, Navy SEALs, after he was captured, unarmed and undefended, in Operation Geronimo.

Today is a rather ordinary day. The press reports terrorist attacks that killed dozens of civilians in Afghanistan, thirty-four more in Pakistan, and eleven in Iraq, where, as was just reported, the regular toll of about ten killed a day increased by 28 percent in May over April. The United Nations reported that May was the worst month for civilian casualties in Afghanistan since records began to be kept four years ago.[1]

A few months earlier, in December, the International Committee of the Red Cross (ICRC) called a rare news conference "to express deep concern that Afghanistan security had deteriorated to its worst point since the overthrow of the Taliban nine years ago and was preventing aid groups from reaching victims of conflict." The head of the Afghanistan office, Reto Stocker, said that the ICRC is "extremely concerned of yet another year of fighting with dramatic consequences for an ever growing number of people in by now almost the entire country." He added that by every measure that the ICRC tracks, the situation has worsened throughout the country. The number of internally displaced people rose by 25 percent last year. Stocker added that "the Red Cross might be undercounting because it could no longer travel to many parts of the country."[2]

This grim analysis was confirmed shortly after by the outgoing UN deputy special representative of the Secretary General for Afghanistan, Robert Watkins. He reported that the "security situation in Afghanistan has worsened to its lowest point since the toppling of the Taliban a decade ago and attacks on aid workers are at unprecedented levels." Before the surge in NATO (that is, US) forces last year, he said, the insurgency was centered in the south and south-east of the country, but since the surge "we have seen the insurgency move to parts of the country where we've never seen [it] before," UN relief agencies now have regular access to just 30 percent of the country, with mixed access for another 30 percent and hardly any for the remaining 40 percent.[3]

Meanwhile the vicious Sunni-Shi'ite conflict that was ignited by the US-UK invasion of Iraq has since spread to the region more generally, with dire consequences and possibly worse to come.[4]

The most dangerous case is Pakistan. One of the leading specialists on Pakistan, British military historian

Anatol Lieven, writes that the war in Afghanistan is "destabilizing and radicalizing Pakistan, risking a geopolitical catastrophe for the United States—and the world—which would dwarf anything that could possibly occur in Afghanistan." At every level of society, he writes, Pakistanis overwhelmingly sympathize with the Afghan Taliban, not because they like them but because "the Taliban are seen as a legitimate force of resistance against an alien occupation of the country," much as the Mujahadeen were perceived when they resisted the Russian occupation in the 1980s. These feelings are shared by the military, who bitterly resent US pressures to sacrifice themselves for Washington's war against the Taliban. Further bitterness is caused by the terror attacks (drones) by the US within Pakistan, sharply accelerated by Obama, and demands by the US that the Pakistani army carry Washington's war into tribal areas of Pakistan that had been pretty much left on their own, even under British rule. The military is the one stable institution in Pakistan, holding the country together. US actions might "provoke a mutiny of parts of the military," Lieven writes, in which case "the Pakistani state would collapse very quickly indeed, with all the disasters this would entail."

The potential disasters are heightened drastically by the fact that Pakistan has a huge and rapidly growing nuclear weapons arsenal, and also a substantial Jihadi movement. Both of these are legacies of the Reagan administration, which pretended it did not know that Zia ul-Haq, the most vicious of Pakistan's military dictators and a Washington favorite, was developing nuclear weapons and was also carrying out a program of radical Islamization of Pakistan with Saudi funding. The potential catastrophe lurking in the background is that these two legacies might combine, with fissile materials leaking into the hands of Jihadis, in which case we might see nuclear weapons (most likely "dirty bombs") exploding in London and New York. Lieven summarizes by remarking that "U.S. and British soldiers are in effect dying in Afghanistan in order to make the world more dangerous for American and British peoples."[5]

The threat that US operations in what has been christened "Afpak"—Afghanistan-Pakistan—might destabilize and radicalize Pakistan is surely understood in Washington. The most significant documents to have been released so far from Wikileaks are the cables from Islamabad from US Ambassador Patterson, who supports US actions in Afpak but warns that they "risk destabilizing the Pakistani state, alienating both the civilian government and military leadership, and provoking a broader governance crisis in Pakistan without finally achieving the goal," and that there is a possibility that "someone working in [Pakistani government] facilities could gradually smuggle enough fissile material out to eventually make a weapon," a danger enhanced by "the vulnerability of weapons in transit."[6]

A few weeks ago the tortured corpse of Pakistani journalist Syed Saleem Shahzad was found, probably murdered by the ISI, Pakistan's powerful intelligence services. Shahzad was a highly regarded (and immensely courageous) investigative reporter who had been exposing how militants were "taking hold of some of Pakistan's most powerful institutions, in particular the military." His murder, it is generally assumed, was a reaction to his exposures of what is recognized to be a "nightmare scenario," steadily being brought closer to reality, with full awareness, by the Obama-Petraeus Afpak strategy.[7]

For such reasons as these, the most immediate and significant consequences of the bin Laden assassination are likely to be in Pakistan. There is much discussion of Washington's anger that Pakistan didn't turn over bin Laden. Less is said about the fury in Pakistan that the US invaded their territory to carry out a political assassination. Anti-American fervor had already reached a very high peak in Pakistan, and these events are already exacerbating it.

The US commandos who carried out the assassination were under orders to fight their way out if necessary. Had that happened, they would surely have received air and maybe ground from US military forces, leading to a confrontation with the Pakistani army. Lieven writes that the Pakistani army is dedicated to protecting the sovereignty of Pakistan, and "if the US ever put Pakistani soldiers in a position where they felt that honour and patriotism required them to fight America, many would be very glad to do so." If the likely disintegration of Pakistan followed, he concludes, an "absolutely inevitable result would be the flow of large numbers of highly trained ex-soldiers, including explosive experts and engineers, to extremist groups." That is the primary threat he sees of leakage of fissile materials to Jihadi hands, a horrendous eventuality.[8]

The Pakistani military had already been pushed to the edge by US attacks on Pakistani sovereignty, including Obama's drone attacks—which he escalated immediately after the killing of bin Laden, rubbing salt in the wounds. As noted, that is in addition to the demand that the Pakistani military cooperate in the US war against the Taliban in Afghanistan, whom the overwhelming majority of Pakistanis, the military included, see as fighting a just war of resistance against an invading army.

US correspondents in Afpak are aware of the rising threat to security that has been enhanced by the bin Laden assassination. Jane Perlez reports the view of "a well-informed Pakistani," close to the top military command, that "a colonels' coup, while unlikely, was not out of the question" after the assassination. "An American military official involved with Pakistan for many years" concurs in this judgment. The result could be that army chief General Ashfaq Parvez Kayani, "the most powerful man in the country," will be replaced by "a more uncompromising anti-American army chief," commanding soldiers who are already "almost uniformly anti-American." The Pakistani military-intelligence complex wasted little time reacting to the assassination. The ISI "arrested five Pakistani informants who helped the Central Intelligence Agency before the Bin Laden raid," according to US officials. The top Army commanders, who run the military by consensus, demanded "that General Kayani get much tougher with the Americans, even edging toward a break, Pakistanis who follow the army closely said." The commanders issued a statement that condemned drone attacks anywhere in Pakistan as "not acceptable under any circumstances." The military authorities had "already blocked the supply of food and water to the base used for the drones, a senior

American official said, adding that they were gradually 'strangling the alliance' by making things difficult for the Americans in Pakistan."[9]

A number of analysts have observed that although bin Laden was finally killed, he won some major successes in his war against the US. "He repeatedly asserted that the only way to drive the U.S. from the Muslim world and defeat its satraps was by drawing Americans into a series of small but expensive wars that would ultimately bankrupt them." Eric Margolis writes. "'Bleeding the U.S.,' in his words. The United States, first under George W. Bush and then Barack Obama, rushed right into bin Laden's trap. . . . Grotesquely overblown military outlays and debt addiction . . . may be the most pernicious legacy of the man who thought he could defeat the United States"[10]—particularly when the debt is being cynically exploited by the far right, with collusion of the Democrat establishment, to undermine what remains of social programs, public education, unions, and, in general, remaining barriers to corporate tyranny, a different topic I cannot pursue here.

That Washington was bent on fulfilling bin Laden's fervent wishes was evident at once. As discussed in the text below, written shortly after 9/11, anyone with knowledge of the region could recognize "that a massive assault on a Muslim population would be the answer to the prayers of bin Laden and his associates, and would lead the U.S. and its allies into a 'diabolical trap,' as the French foreign minister put it." The senior CIA analyst responsible for tracking Osama bin Laden from 1996, Michael Scheuer, wrote shortly after that "bin Laden has been precise in telling

America the reasons he is waging war on us. [He] is out to drastically alter U.S. and Western policies toward the Islamic world," and largely succeeded: "U.S. forces and policies are completing the radicalization of the Islamic world, something Osama bin Laden has been trying to do with substantial but incomplete success since the early 1990s. As a result, I think it is fair to conclude that the United States of America remains bin Laden's only indispensable ally."[11] And arguably remains so, even after his death.

Was there an alternative? There is every likelihood that the Jihadi movement, much of it highly critical of bin Laden, could have been split and undermined after 9/11. The "crime against humanity," as it was rightly called, could have been approached as a crime, with an international operation to apprehend the likely suspects. That was recognized at the time, but no such idea was even considered. It might also have been possible to follow the precedent of law-abiding states, like Nicaragua's response to the massive US terrorist war to which it was subjected (discussed in the text below). Again, unthinkable.

In *9-11*, I quoted Robert Fisk's conclusion that the "horrendous crime" of 9/11 was committed with "wickedness and awesome cruelty,"[12] an accurate judgment. It is useful to bear in mind that the crimes could have been even worse. Suppose, for example, that the attack had gone as far as bombing the White House, killing the president, imposing a brutal military dictatorship that killed thousands and tortured tens of thousands while establishing an international terror center that helped impose similar torture-and-terror states elsewhere and carried out an international assassination campaign; and as an extra fillip, brought in a team of economists—call them "the Kandahar boys"—who quickly drove the economy into one of the worst depressions in its history. That, plainly, would have been a lot worse than 9/11.

Unfortunately, it is not a thought experiment. It happened. The only inaccuracy in this brief account is that the numbers should be multiplied by twenty-five to yield per capita equivalents, the appropriate measure. I am, of course, referring to what in Latin America is often called "the first 9/11": September 11, 1973, when the US succeeded in its intensive efforts to overthrow the democratic government of Salvador Allende in Chile with a military coup that placed General Pinochet's brutal regime in office. One way to get a sense of it today is to visit the Villa Grimaldi in Santiago with one of the rare survivors as a guide, who can describe the exquisite torture regime stage by stage, with doctors attending to ensure that the subject survives to the next and more horrific stage until almost inevitable death. An experience not easily forgotten. The goal, in the words of the Nixon administration, was to kill the "virus"[13] that might encourage all those "foreigners [who] are out to screw us" to take over their own resources and in other ways to pursue an intolerable policy of independent development. In the background was the conclusion of the National Security Council that if the US could not control Latin America, it could not expect "to achieve a successful order elsewhere in the world."[14] Washington's "credibility" would be undermined, as Henry Kissinger put it.

The first 9/11, unlike the second, did not change the world. It was "nothing of very great consequence," as Henry Kissinger assured his boss a few days later.[15]

These events of little consequence were not limited to the military coup that destroyed Chilean democracy and set in motion the horror story that followed. The first 9/11 was just one act in a drama, amply reviewed elsewhere, which began in 1962, when John F. Kennedy shifted the mission of the Latin American military from "hemispheric defense"—an anachronistic holdover from World War II—to "internal security," a concept with a chilling interpretation in US-dominated Latin American circles. The consequences are outlined by Charles Maechling, who led US counterinsurgency and internal defense planning from 1961 to 1966. He described Kennedy's 1962 decision as a shift from toleration "of the rapacity and cruelty of the Latin American military" to "direct complicity" in their crimes, to US support for "the methods of Heinrich Himmler's extermination squads." In the recently published Cambridge University *History of the Cold War*, Latin American scholar John Coatsworth writes that from that time to "the Soviet collapse in 1990, the numbers of political prisoners, torture victims, and executions of non-violent political dissenters in Latin America vastly exceeded those in the Soviet Union and its East European satellites,"[16] including many religious martyrs and mass slaughter as well, always supported or initiated in Washington. The last major violent act was the brutal murder of six leading Latin American intellectuals, Jesuit priests, a few days after the Berlin Wall fell. The perpetrators were an elite Salvadoran battalion, who had already left a shocking trail of blood, fresh from renewed training at the JFK School of Special Warfare, acting on direct orders of the high command of the US client state. That act also framed a decade, which opened with the assassination of Archbishop Romero, the "voice for the voiceless," by much the same hands, while he was reading mass.

The consequences of this hemispheric plague still of course reverberate.

All of this, and much more like it, is dismissed as of little consequence, and forgotten. Those whose mission it is to rule the world enjoy a more comforting picture, articulated well enough in the current issue of the prestigious (and valuable) journal of the Royal Institute of International Affairs in London. The lead article discusses "the visionary international order" of the "second half of the twentieth century" marked by "the universalization of an American vision of commercial prosperity."[17] There is something to that account, but it does not quite convey the perception of those at the wrong end of the guns.

The same is true of the assassination of Osama bin Laden, which brings to an end at least a phase in the "war on terror" re-declared by President George W. Bush on the second 9/11.[18] Let us turn to a few thoughts on that event and its significance.[19]

On May 1, 2011, Osama bin Laden was killed in his virtually unprotected compound by a raiding mission of seventy-nine Navy SEALs, who entered Pakistan by helicopter. After many lurid stories were provided by the government and withdrawn, official reports made it increasingly clear that the operation was a planned assassination, multiply violating elementary norms of international law, beginning with the invasion itself.

There appears to have been no attempt to apprehend the unarmed victim, as presumably could have been done by seventy-nine commandos facing no opposition—except, they report, from his wife, also unarmed, who they shot in self-defense when she "lunged" at them, according to the White House.

A plausible reconstruction of the events is provided by veteran Middle East correspondent Yochi Dreazen and colleagues in the *Atlantic*. Dreazen, formerly the military correspondent for the *Wall Street Journal*, is senior correspondent for the National Journal Group covering military affairs and national security. According to their investigation, White House planning appears not to have considered the option of capturing bin Laden alive: "The administration had made clear to the military's clandestine Joint Special Operations Command that it wanted bin Laden dead, according to a senior U.S. official with knowledge of the discussions. A high-ranking military officer briefed on the assault said the SEALs knew their mission was not to take him alive."

The authors add: "For many at the Pentagon and the Central Intelligence Agency who had spent nearly a decade hunting bin Laden, killing the militant was a necessary and justified act of vengeance." Furthermore, "Capturing bin Laden alive would have also presented the administration with an array of nettlesome legal and political challenges." Better, then, to assassinate him, dumping his body into the sea without the autopsy considered essential after a killing, whether considered justified or not—an act that predictably provoked both anger and skepticism in much of the Muslim world.

As the *Atlantic* inquiry observes, "The decision to kill bin Laden outright was the clearest illustration to date of a little-noticed aspect of the Obama administration's counterterror policy. The Bush administration captured thousands of suspected militants and sent them to detention camps in Afghanistan, Iraq, and Guantanamo Bay. The Obama administration, by contrast, has focused on eliminating individual terrorists rather than attempting to take them alive." That is one significant difference between Bush and Obama. The authors quote former West German Chancellor Helmut Schmidt, who "told German TV that the U.S. raid was 'quite clearly a violation of international law' and that bin Laden should have been detained and put on trial," contrasting Schmidt with US Attorney General Eric Holder, who "defended the decision to kill bin Laden although he didn't pose an immediate threat to the Navy SEALs, telling a House panel . . . that the assault had been 'lawful, legitimate and appropriate in every way.'"[20]

The disposal of the body without autopsy was also criticized by allies. The highly regarded British barrister Geoffrey Robertson, who supported the intervention and opposed the execution largely on pragmatic grounds, nevertheless described Obama's claim that "justice was done" as an "absurdity" that should have been obvious to a former professor of constitutional law.[21] Pakistan law "requires a colonial inquest on violent death, and international human rights law insists that the 'right to life' mandates an inquiry whenever violent death occurs from government or police action. The U.S. is therefore under a duty to hold an inquiry that will satisfy the world as to the true circumstances of this killing." Robertson adds that "The law permits criminals to be shot in self-defense if they (or their accomplices) resist arrest in ways that endanger those striving to apprehend them. They should, if possible, be given the opportunity to surrender, but even if they do not come out with their hands up, they must be taken alive if that can be achieved without risk. Exactly how bin Laden came to be 'shot in the head' (especially if it was the back of his head, execution-style) therefore requires explanation. Why a hasty 'burial at sea' without a post mortem, as the law requires?"

Robertson attributes the murder to "America's obsessive belief in capital punishment—alone among advanced nations—[which] is reflected in its rejoicing at the manner of bin Laden's demise"—though some who held that "The killing of Osama bin Laden was a just and necessary undertaking" expressed no joy while applauding the murder of a defenseless prisoner by an elite commando team facing no threat.[22]

Robertson usefully reminds us that "It was not always thus. When the time came to consider the fate of men much more steeped in wickedness than Osama bin Laden—namely the Nazi leadership—the British government wanted them hanged within six hours of capture. President Truman demurred, citing the conclusion of Justice Robert Jackson that summary execution 'would not sit easily on the American conscience or be remembered by our children with pride . . . the only course is to determine the innocence or guilt of the accused after a hearing as dispassionate as the times will permit and upon a record that will leave our reasons and motives clear.'"

The editors of the *Daily Beast* comment that "The joy is understandable, but to many outsiders, unattractive. It endorses what looks increasingly like a cold-blooded assassination as the White House is now forced to admit that Osama bin Laden was unarmed when he was shot twice in the head."[23]

Eric Margolis comments that "Washington has never made public the evidence of its claim that Osama bin Laden was behind the 9/11 attacks," presumably one reason why "Polls show that fully a third of American respondents believe that the U.S. government and/or Israel were behind 9/11" while in the Muslim world skepticism is much higher. "An open trial in the U.S. or at the Hague would have exposed these claims to the light of day," he continues, a practical reason why Washington should have followed the law.[24]

In societies that profess some respect for law, suspects are apprehended and brought to fair trial. I stress "suspects." In June 2002, FBI head Robert Mueller, in what the *Washington Post* described as "among his most detailed public comments on the origins of the attacks," could say only that "investigators believe the idea of the Sept. 11 attacks on the World Trade Center and Pentagon came from al Qaeda leaders in Afghanistan, the actual plotting was done in Germany, and the financing came through the United Arab Emirates from sources in Afghanistan." In his own words, "We think the masterminds of it were in Afghanistan, high in the al Qaeda leadership. Plotters and others—the principals—came together in Germany and perhaps elsewhere."[25] What the FBI believed and thought in June 2002 they didn't know eight months earlier, when Washington dismissed tentative offers by the Taliban (how serious, we do not know) to permit a trial of bin Laden if they were presented with evidence. Thus it is not true, as President Obama claimed in his White House statement, that "We quickly learned that the 9/11 attacks were carried out by al Qaeda."

There has never been any reason to doubt what the FBI believed in mid-2002, but that leaves us far from the proof of guilt required in civilized societies—and whatever the evidence might be, it does not warrant murdering a suspect who could, it seems, have been easily apprehended and brought to trial. Much the same is true of evidence provided since. Thus the 9/11 Commission provided extensive circumstantial evidence of bin Laden's role in 9/11, based primarily on what it had been told about confessions by prisoners in Guantanamo. It is doubtful that much of that would hold up in an independent court, considering the ways confessions were elicited. But in any event, the conclusions of a congressionally authorized investigation, however convincing one finds them, plainly fall short of a sentence by a credible court, which is what shifts the category of the accused from suspect to convicted. There is much talk of bin Laden's "confession," but that was a boast, not a confession, with as much credibility as my "confession" that I won the Boston marathon. The boast tells us a lot about his character, but nothing about his responsibility for what he regarded as a great achievement, for which he wanted to take credit.

Again, all of this is, transparently, quite independent of one's judgments about his responsibility, which seemed clear immediately, even before the FBI inquiry, and still does.

It is worth adding that bin Laden's responsibility was recognized in much of the Muslim world, and condemned. One significant example is the distinguished Lebanese cleric Sheikh Fadlallah, greatly respected by Hizbollah and Shia groups generally, outside Lebanon as well. He had some experience with assassinations. He had been targeted for assassination: by a truck bomb outside a mosque, in a CIA-organized operation in 1985. He escaped, but eighty others were killed, mostly women and girls as they left the mosque—one of those innumerable crimes that do not enter the annals of terror because of the fallacy of "wrong agency." Sheikh Fadlallah sharply condemned the 9/11 attacks, as did many other leading figures in the Muslim world, within the Jihadi movement as well. Among others, the head of Hizbollah, Sayyed Hassan Nasrallah, sharply condemned bin Laden and Jihadi ideology.[26]

One of the leading specialists on the Jihadi movement, Fawaz Gerges, suggests that the movement might have been split at that time had the US exploited the opportunity instead of mobilizing the movement, particularly by the attack on Iraq, a great boon to bin Laden, which led to a sharp increase in terror, as intelligence agencies had anticipated. That they had anticipated it, which was already clear enough at the time, was confirmed by the former head of Britain's domestic intelligence agency MI5 at the Chilcot hearings investigating the background for the war. Confirming other analyses, she testified that both British and US intelligence were aware that Saddam posed no serious threat and that the invasion was likely to increase terror; and that the invasions of Iraq and Afghanistan had radicalized parts of a generation of Muslims who saw the military actions as an "attack on Islam."[27] As is often the case, security was not a high priority for state action.

It might be instructive to ask ourselves how we would be reacting if Iraqi command=os landed at George W. Bush's compound, assassinated him, and dumped his body in the Atlantic (after proper burial rites, of course). Uncontroversially, he is not a "suspect" but the "decider" who gave the orders to invade Iraq—that is, to commit the "supreme international crime differing only from other war crimes in that it contains within itself the accumulated evil of the whole" for which Nazi criminals were hanged: the hundreds of thousands of deaths, millions of refugees, destruction of much of the country and the national heritage, and the murderous sectarian conflict that has now spread to the rest of the region. Equally uncontroversially, these crimes vastly exceed anything attributed to bin Laden.

To say that all of this is uncontroversial, as it is, is not to imply that it is not denied. The existence of flat earthers does not change the fact that, uncontroversially, the earth is not flat. Similarly, it is uncontroversial that Stalin and Hitler were responsible for horrendous crimes, though loyalists deny it. All of this should, again, be too obvious for comment, and would be, except in an atmosphere of hysteria so extreme that it blocks rational thought.

Similarly, it is uncontroversial that Bush and associates did commit the "supreme international crime," the crime of aggression. The crime was defined clearly enough by Justice Robert Jackson, Chief of Counsel for the United States at Nuremberg, reiterated in an authoritative General Assembly resolution. An "aggressor," Jackson proposed to the Tribunal in his opening statement, is a state that is the first to commit such actions as "Invasion of its armed forces, with or without a declaration of war, of the territory of another State. . . ." No one, even the most extreme supporter of the aggression, denies that Bush and associates did just that.

We might also do well to recall Jackson's eloquent words at Nuremberg on the principle of universality: "If certain acts of violation of treaties are crimes, they are crimes whether the United States does them or whether Germany does them, and we are not prepared to lay down a rule of criminal conduct against others which we would not be willing to have invoked against us." And elsewhere: "We must never forget that the record on which we judge these defendants is the record on which history will judge us tomorrow. To pass these defendants a poisoned chalice is to put it to our own lips as well."[28]

It is also clear that announced intentions are irrelevant, even if they are truly believed. Internal records reveal that

Japanese fascists apparently did believe that by ravaging China they were laboring to turn it into an "earthly paradise." We don't know whether Hitler believed that he was defending Germany from the "wild terror" of the Poles, or was taking over Czechoslovakia to protect its population from ethnic conflict and provide them with the benefits of a superior culture, or was saving the glories of the civilization of the Greeks from barbarians of East and West, as his acolytes claimed (Martin Heidegger). And although it may be difficult to imagine, it is conceivable that Bush and company believed that they were protecting the world from destruction by Saddam's nuclear weapons. All irrelevant, though ardent loyalists on all sides may try to convince themselves otherwise.

We are left with two choices: either Bush and associates are guilty of the "supreme international crime" including all the evils that follow, crimes that go vastly beyond anything attributed to bin Laden; or else we declare that the Nuremberg proceedings were a farce and that the allies were guilty of judicial murder. Again, that is entirely independent of the question of the guilt of those charged: established by the Nuremberg Tribunal in the case of the Nazi criminals, plausibly surmised from the outset in the case of bin Laden, though the opportunity to prove the case in court was withdrawn by Obama.

A few days before the bin Laden assassination, Orlando Bosch died peacefully in Florida, where he resided along with his accomplice Luis Posada Carilles and many other associates in international terrorism. After he was accused of dozens of terrorist crimes by the FBI, Bosch was granted a presidential pardon by Bush I over the objections of the Justice Department, which found the conclusion "inescapable that it would be prejudicial to the public interest for the United States to provide a safe haven for Bosch."[28] The coincidence of deaths at once calls to mind the Bush II doctrine, which has "already become a de facto rule of international relations," according to the noted Harvard international relations specialist Graham Allison. The doctrine revokes "the sovereignty of states that provide sanctuary to terrorists," Allison writes, referring to the pronouncement of Bush II, directed to the Taliban, that "those who harbor terrorists are as guilty as the terrorists themselves." Such states, therefore, have lost their sovereignty and are fit targets for bombing and terror; for example, the state that harbored Bosch and his associates. When Bush issued this new "de facto rule of international relations," no one seemed to notice that he was calling for invasion and destruction of the US and murder of its criminal presidents.[30]

None of this is problematic, of course, if we reject Justice Jackson's principle of universality, and adopt instead the principle that the US is self-immunized against international law and conventions—as, in fact, the government has frequently made very clear, an important fact, much too little understood.

It is also worth thinking about the name given to the operation: Operation Geronimo. The imperial mentality is so profound that few seem able to perceive that the White House is glorifying bin Laden by calling him "Geronimo"—the Apache Indian chief who led the courageous resistance to the invaders who sought to consign his people to the fate of "that hapless race of native Americans, which we are exterminating with such merciless and perfidious cruelty, among the heinous sins of this nation, for which I believe God will one day bring [it] to judgement," in the words of the great grand strategist John Quincy Adams, the intellectual architect of manifest destiny, long after his own contributions to these sins had passed. Some did comprehend, not surprisingly. The remnants of that hapless race protested vigorously. The same was true elsewhere, notably in Mexico, where there was great outrage and disbelief—among people who have not forgotten that the "heinous sin" was carried out in territories stolen from Mexico in a war of aggression.

The casual choice of the name is reminiscent of the ease with which we name our murder weapons after victims of our crimes: Apache, Blackhawk, Tomahawk. . . . We might react differently if the Luftwaffe were to call its fighter planes "Jew" and "Gypsy."

The examples mentioned would fall under the category of "American exceptionalism," were it not for the fact that easy suppression of one's own crimes is virtually ubiquitous among powerful states, at least those that are not defeated and forced to acknowledge reality. Other current illustrations are too numerous to mention. To take just one, of great current significance, consider Obama's terror weapons (drones) in Pakistan. Suppose that during the 1980s, when they were occupying Afghanistan, the Russians had carried out targeted assassinations in Pakistan aimed at those who were financing, arming, and training the insurgents—quite proudly and openly. For example, targeting the CIA station chief in Islamabad, who explained that he "loved" the "noble goal" of his mission: to "kill Soviet Soldiers . . . not to liberate Afghanistan."

There is no need to imagine the reaction, but there is a crucial distinction: That was *them*, this is *us*.

What are the likely consequences of the killing of bin Laden? For the Arab world, it will probably mean little. He had long been a fading presence, and in the past few months was eclipsed by the Arab Spring. His significance in the Arab world is captured by the headline in the *New York Times* for an op-ed by Middle East/al Qaeda specialist Gilles Kepel; "Bin Laden was Dead Already" (May 7). Kepel writes that few in the Arab world are likely to care. That headline might have been dated far earlier, had the US not mobilized the Jihadi movement by the attacks on Afghanistan and Iraq, as suggested by the intelligence agencies and scholarship. As for the Jihadi movement, within it bin Laden was doubtless a venerated symbol, but apparently did not play much more of a role for this "network of networks," as analysts call it, which undertake mostly independent operations.

As already discussed, Operation Geronimo might have been the spark that set off a conflagration in Pakistan, with dire consequences. Perhaps the assassination was perceived by the administration as an "act of vengeance," as Robertson concludes.[31] And perhaps the rejection of the legal option of a trial reflects a difference between the moral culture of 1945 and today, as he suggests. Whatever the motive was, it could hardly have been security. As in the case of the "supreme international crime" in Iraq, the bin

Laden assassination is another illustration of the important fact that security is often not a high priority for state action, contrary to received doctrine.

There is much more to say, but even the most obvious and elementary facts should provide us with a good deal to think about when we consider 9/11 and its consequences, and what they portend for the future.

NOTES

1. Faris Ali, "Suspected Suicide Bombing Kills 34 in Pakistan," Reuters, June 11, 2011, http://www.reuters.com/article/2011/06/11/us-pakistan-blasts-idUSTRE75A1TQ20110611; "Bombings Kill Dozens in Pakistan," *New York Times*, June 11, 2011, http://www.nytimes.com/2011/06/12/world/asia/12peshawar.html?ref=world; Hashim Shukoor, "At Least 21 Killed in Afghanistan Attacks," *Truthout,* June 11, 2011, http://www.truth-out.org/least-21-killed-afghanistan-attacks/1307889681; Jack Healy, "Car Bombings and Shooting of Family Kill 11 in Iraq," *New York Times*, June 11, 2011, http://www.nytimes.com/2011/06/12/world/middleeast/12iraq.html?_r=1&ref=world.

2. Alissa Rubin, "For Red Cross, Aid Conditions Hit New Low in Afghanistan," *New York Times*, Dec. 16, 2010, http://www.nytimes.com/2010/12/16/world/asia/16redcross.html?_r=1.

3. "Afghan Security Worse in a Decade: UN," *ABC News*, February 24, 2011, http://www.abc.net.au/news/stories/2011/02/24/3147163.htm.

4. See Nir Rosen, *Aftermath: Following the Bloodshed of America's Wars in the Muslim World* (Nation Books, 2010).

5. Anatol Lieven, "A Mutiny Grows in Punjab," *National Interest*, March/April 2011, http://nationalinterest.org/article/mutiny-grows-punjab-4889.

6. The fullest discussion of this critically important material is by Fred Branfman, who had exposed the grotesque US war against the peasants of northern Laos at the time; "Wikileaks Exposes the Danger of Pakistan's Nukes," *Truthdig*, January 13, 2011, http://www.truthdig.com/report/item/wikileaks_exposes_the_danger_of_pakistans_nukes_20110113/.

7. "James Lamont and Farhan Bokhari, "Murder of Pakistani journalist raises awkward questions inside the regime," *Financial Times*, June 3, 2011, http://www.ft.com/cms/s/0/7b440aae-8e08-11e0-bee5-00144feab49a.html#axzz1PwOPdzye.

8. Lieven, *Pakistan: A Hard Country* (Public Affairs, 2011).

9. Jane Perlez, "Pakistan's Chief of Army Fights to Keep His Job," *New York Times*, June 15, 2011, http://www.nytimes.com/2011/06/16/world/asia/16pakistan.html?pagewanted=1&_r=1&hp.

10. Eric Margolis, "Osama's Ghost," *American Conservative*, May 20, 2011, http://www.amconmag.com/blog/osamas-ghost/.

11. Anonymous (Michael Scheuer), *Imperial Hubris: Why the West is Losing the War on Terror* (Washington DC: Potomac, 2004).

12. Noam Chomsky, *9-11* (New York: Seven Stories Press 2001) 45–46.

13. Armand Toprani and Richard Moss, "Filling the Three-Year Gap: Nixon, Allende, and the White House Tapes, 1971–73," *Passport: The Newsletter of the Society for Historians of American Foreign Relations* 41, no. 3 (2011): 4–5.

14. David Schmitz, *Thank God They're on Our Side* (Chapel Hill, NC: The University of North Carolina Press, 1999).

15. Lubna Z. Qureshi, *Nixon, Kissinger, and Allende: US Involvement in the 1973 Coup in Chile* (Landham, MD: Lexington Books, 2009).

16. John Coatsworth, "The Cold War in Central America, 1975–1991," in *History of the Cold War* Vol. 3 (Cambridge: Cambridge University Press 2010).

17. Harold James, "International Order after the Financial Crisis," *International Affairs* 87, no. 3 (2011): 525–537.

18. The first war on terror was declared by the Reagan administration, which came into office announcing that a primary focus of foreign policy would be state-directed international terrorism, "the plague of the modern age," "a return to barbarism in our time," and so on. The impressive rhetoric had considerable merit, though not exactly as intended. The toll of Reagan's war on terror included hundreds of thousands of corpses in Central America, over a million in Angola and Mozambique where Reagan was strongly supporting the apartheid South African regime in its defense against "one of the more notorious terrorist groups" in the world (1988, Nelson Mandela's African National Congress), tens of thousands in the Middle East, and much else. All dispatched to the memory hole along with other matters of little consequence.

19. I know of no comprehensive study, but it seems quite clear that reactions were considerably different in the West and the Global South, where events of little consequence tend to be remembered. The remarks that follow are adapted from my comments shortly after the assassination, at http://www.zcommunications.org/there-is-much-more-to-say-by-noam-chomsky.

20. Yochi Dreazen, Aamer Madhani, and Marc Ambinder, "Goal Was Never to Capture bin Laden; The Navy SEALs Knew Their Mission was to Kill the al Qaeda Leader, Not Take Him Alive," *The Atlantic*, May 3, 2011, http://www.theatlantic.com/politics/archive/2011/05/goal-was-never-to-capture-bin-laden/238330/.

21. Geoffrey Robertson, "Bin Laden Should Have Been Captured, Not Killed," *Daily Beast* accessed through Yahoo! News, accessed on June 23, 2011, http://news.yahoo.com/s/dailybeast/20110503/ts_dailybeast/13863_osamabinladendeathwhyheshouldhavebeencapturednotkilled_1.

22. Eric Alterman, "Bin Gotten," *The Nation*, May 23, 2011.

23. Robertson, *Daily Beast*, 2011.

24. Margolis, *American Conservative*, 2011.

25. Walter Pincus, "Mueller Outlines Origin, Funding of Sept. 11 Plot," *Washington Post*, June 6, 2002.

26. Fawaz A. Gerges, *The Far Enemy: Why Jihad Went Global* (Cambridge, 2005, 2009); Gerges, *Journey of the Jihadist: Inside Muslim Militancy* (Harcourt, 2006).

27. Haroon Siddique, "Iraq inquiry: Saddam posed very limited threat to UK, ex-MI5 chief says," *Guardian*, July 20, 2010, http://www.guardian.co.uk/uk/2010/jul/20/iraq-inquiry-saddam-mi5-chief.

28. The preceding four quotes can be cited in "The International Tribunal for Germany: Contents of the Nuremberg Trials Collection," *The Avalon Project: Documents in Law, History, and Diplomacy*, 2008, http://avalon.law.yale.edu/subject_menus/imt.asp.

29. Associate Attorney General Joe D. Whitley, "Exclusion Proceeding for Orlando Bosch Avila," US Department of Justice, file A28 851 622, A11 861 810.

30. Graham Allison, "How to Stop Nuclear Terror," *Foreign Affairs*, January/February 2004.

31. Robertson, *Daily Beast*, 2011.

9-11

1.

Not Since the War of 1812

Based on an interview with *Il Manifesto* (Italy),
September 19, 2001.

Q: The fall of the Berlin Wall didn't claim any victims, but it did profoundly change the geopolitical scene. Do you think that the attacks of 9-11 could have a similar effect?

CHOMSKY: The fall of the Berlin Wall was an event of great importance and did change the geopolitical scene, but not in the ways usually assumed, in my opinion. I've tried to explain my reasons elsewhere and won't go into it now.

The horrifying atrocities of September 11 are something quite new in world affairs, not in their scale and character, but in the target. For the United States, this is the first time since the War of 1812 that the national territory has been under attack, or even threatened. Many commentators have brought up a Pearl Harbor analogy, but that is misleading. On December 7, 1941, military bases in two U.S. colonies were attacked—not the national territory, which was never threatened. The U.S. preferred to call Hawaii a "territory," but it was in effect a colony. During the past several hundred years the U.S. annihilated the indigenous population (millions of people), conquered half of Mexico (in fact, the territories of indigenous peoples, but that is another matter), intervened violently in the surrounding region, conquered Hawaii and the Philippines (killing hundreds of thousands of Filipinos), and, in the past half century particularly, extended its resort to force throughout much of the world. The number of victims is colossal. For the first time, the guns have been directed the other way. That is a dramatic change.

The same is true, even more dramatically, of Europe. Europe has suffered murderous destruction, but from internal wars. Meanwhile European powers conquered much of the world with extreme brutality. With the rarest of exceptions, they were not under attack by their foreign victims. England was not attacked by India, nor Belgium by the Congo, nor Italy by Ethiopia, nor France by Algeria (also not regarded by France as "a colony"). It is not surprising, therefore, that Europe should be utterly shocked by the terrorist crimes of September 11. Again, not because of the scale, regrettably.

Exactly what this portends, no one can guess. But that it is something strikingly new is quite clear.

My impression is that these attacks won't offer us new political scenery, but that they rather confirm the existence of a problem inside the "Empire." The problem concerns political authority and power. What do you think?

The likely perpetrators are a category of their own, but uncontroversially, they draw support from a reservoir of bitterness and anger over U.S. policies in the region, extending those of earlier European masters. There certainly is an issue of "political authority and power." In the wake of the attacks, the *Wall Street Journal* surveyed opinions of "moneyed Muslims" in the region: bankers, professionals, businessmen with ties to the United States. They expressed dismay and anger about U.S. support for harsh authoritarian states and the barriers that Washington places against independent development and political democracy by its policies of "propping up oppressive regimes." Their primary concern, however, was different: Washington's policies towards Iraq and towards Israel's military occupation. Among the great mass of poor and suffering people, similar sentiments are much more bitter, and they are also hardly pleased to see the wealth of the region flow to the West and to small Western-oriented elites and corrupt and brutal rulers backed by Western power. So there definitely are problems of authority and power. The immediately announced U.S. reaction was to deal with these problems by intensifying them. That is, of course, not inevitable. A good deal depends on the outcome of such considerations.

Is America having trouble governing the process of globalization—and I don't mean just in terms of national security or intelligence systems?

The U.S. doesn't govern the corporate globalization project, though it of course has a primary role. These programs have been arousing enormous opposition, primarily in the

South, where mass protests could often be suppressed or ignored. In the past few years, the protests reached the rich countries as well, and hence became the focus of great concern to the powerful, who now feel themselves on the defensive, not without reason. There are very substantial reasons for the worldwide opposition to the particular form of investor-rights "globalization" that is being imposed, but this is not the place to go into that.

"Intelligent bombs" in Iraq, "humanitarian intervention" in Kosovo. The U.S.A. never used the word "war" to describe that. Now they are talking about war against a nameless enemy. Why?

At first the U.S. used the word "crusade," but it was quickly pointed out that if they hope to enlist their allies in the Islamic world, it would be a serious mistake, for obvious reasons. The rhetoric therefore shifted to "war." The Gulf War of 1991 was called a "war." The bombing of Serbia was called a "humanitarian intervention," by no means a novel usage. That was a standard description of European imperialist ventures in the 19th century. To cite some more recent examples, the major recent scholarly work on "humanitarian intervention" cites three examples of "humanitarian intervention" in the immediate pre-World War II period: Japan's invasion of Manchuria, Mussolini's invasion of Ethiopia, and Hitler's takeover of the Sudetenland. The author of course is not suggesting that the term is apt; rather, that the crimes were masked as "humanitarian."

Whether the Kosovo intervention indeed was "humanitarian," possibly the first such case in history, is a matter of fact: passionate declaration does not suffice, if only because virtually every use of force is justified in these terms. It is quite extraordinary how weak the arguments are to justify the claim of humanitarian intent in the Kosovo case; more accurately, they scarcely exist, and the official government reasons are quite different. But that's a separate matter, which I've written about in some detail elsewhere.

But even the pretext of "humanitarian intervention" cannot be used in the normal way in the present case. So we are left with "war."

The proper term would be "crime"—perhaps "crime against humanity," as Robert Fisk has stressed. But there are laws for punishing crimes: identify the perpetrators, and hold them accountable, the course that is widely recommended in the Middle East, by the Vatican, and many others. But that requires solid evidence, and it opens doors to dangerous questions: to mention only the most obvious one, who were the perpetrators of the crime of international terrorism condemned by the World Court 15 years ago?

For such reasons, it is better to use a vague term, like "war." To call it a "war against terrorism," however, is simply more propaganda, unless the "war" really does target terrorism. But that is plainly not contemplated because Western powers could never abide by their own official definitions of the term, as in the U.S. Code* or Army

---

* "[An] act of terrorism, means any activity that (A) involves a violent act or an act dangerous to human life that is a violation of the criminal laws of the United States or any State, or that would be a criminal violation if committed within the jurisdiction of the United States or of any State; and (B) appears to be intended (i) to intimidate or coerce a civilian population; (ii) to influence the policy of a government by intimidation or coercion; or (iii) to affect the conduct of a government by assassination or kidnapping." *(United States Code Congressional and Administrative News, 98th Congress, Second Session, 1984, Oct. 19, volume 2; par. 3077, 98 STAT. 2707 [West Publishing Co., 1984]).*

manuals. To do so would at once reveal that the U.S. is a leading terrorist state, as are its clients.

Perhaps I may quote political scientist Michael Stohl: "We must recognize that by convention—and it must be emphasized only by convention—great power use and the threat of the use of force is normally described as coercive diplomacy and not as a form of terrorism," though it commonly involves "the threat and often the use of violence for what would be described as terroristic purposes were it not great powers who were pursuing the very same tactic," in accord with the literal meaning of the term. Under the (admittedly unimaginable) circumstances that Western intellectual culture were willing to adopt the literal meaning, the war against terrorism would take quite a different form, along lines spelled out in extensive detail in literature that does not enter the respectable canon.

The quote I just gave is cited in a survey volume called *Western State Terrorism*, edited by Alex George and published by a major publisher 10 years ago, but unmentionable in the United States. Stohl's point is then illustrated in detail throughout the book. And there are many others, extensively documented from the most reliable sources—for example, official government documents—but also unmentionable in the U.S., though the taboo is not so strict in other English-speaking countries, or elsewhere.

NATO is keeping quiet until they find out whether the attack was internal or external. How do you interpret this?

I do not think that that is the reason for NATO's hesitation. There is no serious doubt that the attack was "external." I presume that NATO's reasons for hesitation are those that European leaders are expressing quite publicly.

They recognize, as does everyone with close knowledge of the region, that a massive assault on a Muslim population would be the answer to the prayers of bin Laden and his associates, and would lead the U.S. and its allies into a "diabolical trap," as the French foreign minister put it.

Could you say something about connivance and the role of American secret service?

I don't quite understand the question. This attack was surely an enormous shock and surprise to the intelligence services of the West, including those of the United States. The CIA did have a role, a major one in fact, but that was in the 1980s, when it joined Pakistani intelligence and others (Saudi Arabia, Britain, etc.) in recruiting, training, and arming the most extreme Islamic fundamentalists it could find to fight a "Holy War" against the Russian invaders of Afghanistan.

The best source on this topic is the book *Unholy Wars*, written by longtime Middle East correspondent and author John Cooley. There is now, predictably, an effort under way to clean up the record and pretend that the U.S. was an innocent bystander, and a bit surprisingly, even respectable journals (not to speak of others) are soberly quoting CIA officials to "demonstrate" that required conclusion—in gross violation of the most elementary journalistic standards.

After that war was over, the "Afghanis" (many, like bin Laden, not Afghans), turned their attention elsewhere: for example, to Chechnya and Bosnia, where they may have received at least tacit U.S. support. Not surprisingly, they were welcomed by the governments; in Bosnia, many Islamic volunteers were granted citizenship in gratitude for their military services (Carlotta Gall, *New York Times*, October 2, 2001).

And to western China, where they are fighting for liberation from Chinese domination; these are Chinese Muslims, some apparently sent by China to Afghanistan as early as 1978 to join a guerrilla rebellion against the government, later joining the CIA-organized forces after the Russian invasion in 1979 in support of the government Russia backed—and installed, much as the U.S. installed a government in South Vietnam and then invaded to "defend" the country it was attacking, to cite a fairly close analog. And in the southern Philippines, North Africa, and elsewhere, fighting for the same causes, as they see it. They also turned their attention to their prime enemies Saudi Arabia, Egypt, and other Arab states, and by the 1990s, also to the U.S. (which bin Laden regards as having invaded Saudi Arabia much as Russia invaded Afghanistan).

What consequences do you foresee for the Seattle movement? Do you think it will suffer as a result, or is it possible that it will gain momentum?

It is certainly a setback for the worldwide protests against corporate globalization, which—again—did not begin in

Seattle. Such terrorist atrocities are a gift to the harshest and most repressive elements on all sides, and are sure to be exploited—already have been in fact—to accelerate the agenda of militarization, regimentation, reversal of social democratic programs, transfer of wealth to narrow sectors, and undermining democracy in any meaningful form. But that will not happen without resistance, and I doubt that it will succeed, except in the short term.

What are the consequences for the Middle East? In particular for the Israeli-Palestinian conflict?

The atrocities of September 11 were a devastating blow for the Palestinians, as they instantly recognized. Israel is openly exulting in the "window of opportunity" it now has to crush Palestinians with impunity. In the first few days after the 9-11 attack, Israeli tanks entered Palestinian cities (Jenin, Ramallah, Jericho for the first time), several dozen Palestinians were killed, and Israel's iron grip on the population tightened, exactly as would be expected. Again, these are the common dynamics of a cycle of escalating violence, familiar throughout the world: Northern Ireland, Israel-Palestine, the Balkans, and elsewhere.

How do you judge the reaction of Americans? They seemed pretty cool-headed, but as Saskia Sassen recently said in an interview, "We already feel as though we are at war."

The immediate reaction was shock, horror, anger, fear, a desire for revenge. But public opinion is mixed, and countercurrents did not take long to develop. They are now even being recognized in mainstream commentary. Today's newspapers, for example.

In an interview you gave to the Mexican daily La Jornada, *you said that we are faced with a new type of war. What exactly did you mean?*

It is a new type of war for the reasons mentioned in response to your first question: the guns are now aimed in a different direction, something quite new in the history of Europe and its offshoots.

Are Arabs, by definition, necessarily fundamentalist, the West's new enemy?

Certainly not. First of all, no one with even a shred of rationality defines Arabs as "fundamentalist." Secondly, the U.S. and the West generally have no objection to religious fundamentalism as such. The U.S., in fact, is one of the most extreme religious fundamentalist cultures in the world; not the state, but the popular culture. In the Islamic world, the most extreme fundamentalist state, apart from the Taliban, is Saudi Arabia, a U.S. client state since its origins; the Taliban are in fact an offshoot of the Saudi version of Islam.

Radical Islamist extremists, often called "fundamentalists," were U.S. favorites in the 1980s, because they were the best killers who could be found. In those years, a prime enemy of the U.S. was the Catholic Church, which had sinned grievously in Latin America by adopting "the preferential option for the poor," and suffered bitterly for that crime. The West is quite ecumenical in its choice of enemies. The criteria are subordination and service to power, not religion. There are many other illustrations.

2.

Is the War on Terrorism Winnable?

Based on separate interviews with Kevin Canfield of the *Hartford Courant* on
September 20, 2001, and David Barsamian on September 21, 2001.

*Q: Is the nation's so-called war on terrorism winnable? If
yes, how? If no, then what should the Bush administration
do to prevent attacks like the ones that struck New York and
Washington?*

CHOMSKY: If we want to consider this question seriously, we should recognize that in much of the world the
U.S. is regarded as a leading terrorist state, and with good
reason. We might bear in mind, for example, that in 1986
the U.S. was condemned by the World Court for "unlawful use of force" (international terrorism) and then vetoed
a Security Council resolution calling on all states (meaning
the U.S.) to adhere to international law. Only one of
countless examples.

But to keep to the narrow question—the terrorism of
others directed against us—we know quite well how the
problem should be addressed, if we want to reduce the
threat rather than escalate it. When IRA bombs were set
off in London, there was no call to bomb West Belfast, or

Boston, the source of much of the financial support for the IRA. Rather, steps were taken to apprehend the criminals, and efforts were made to deal with what lay behind the resort to terror. When a federal building was blown up in Oklahoma City, there were calls for bombing the Middle East, and it probably would have happened if the source turned out to be there. When it was found to be domes-tic, with links to the ultra-right militias, there was no call to obliterate Montana and Idaho. Rather, there was a search for the perpetrator, who was found, brought to court, and sentenced, and there were efforts to understand the grievances that lie behind such crimes and to address the problems. Just about every crime—whether a robbery in the streets or colossal atrocities—has reasons, and com-monly we find that some of them are serious and should be addressed.

There are proper and lawful ways to proceed in the case of crimes, whatever their scale. And there are precedents. A clear example is the one I just mentioned, one that should be entirely uncontroversial, because of the reaction of the highest international authorities.

Nicaragua in the 1980s was subjected to violent assault by the U.S. Tens of thousands of people died. The country was substantially destroyed; it may never recover. The international terrorist attack was accompanied by a devas-tating economic war, which a small country isolated by a vengeful and cruel superpower could scarcely sustain, as the leading historians of Nicaragua, Thomas Walker for one, have reviewed in detail. The effects on the country are much more severe even than the tragedies in New York the other day. They didn't respond by setting off bombs in Washington. They went to the World Court, which ruled in their favor, ordering the U.S. to desist and pay substantial reparations. The U.S. dismissed the court judgment with contempt, responding with an immediate escalation of the attack. So Nicaragua then went to the Security Council, which considered a resolution calling on states to observe international law. The U.S. alone vetoed it. They went to the General Assembly, where they got a similar resolution that passed with the U.S. and Israel opposed two years in a row (joined once by El Salvador). That's the way a state should proceed. If Nicaragua had been powerful enough, it could have set up another criminal court. Those are the measures the U.S. could pursue, and nobody's going to block it. That's what they're being asked to do by people throughout the region, including their allies.

Remember, the governments in the Middle East and North Africa, like the terrorist Algerian government, which is one of the most vicious of all, would be happy to join the U.S. in opposing terrorist networks which are attacking them. They're the prime targets. But they have been asking for some evidence, and they want to do it in a framework of at least minimal commitment to international law. The Egyptian position is complex. They're part of the primary system that organized the radical Islamic forces of which the bin Laden network was a part. They were the first victims of it when Sadat was assassinated. They've been major victims of it since. They'd like to crush it, but, they say, only after some evidence is presented about who's involved and within the framework of the UN Charter, under the aegis of the Security Council.

That is the course one follows if the intention is to reduce the probability of further atrocities. There is another course: react with extreme violence, and expect to escalate the cycle of violence, leading to still further atrocities such as the one that is inciting the call for revenge. The dynamic is very familiar.

What aspect or aspects of the story have been underreported by the mainstream press, and why is it important that they be paid more attention?

There are several fundamental questions:

First, what courses of action are open to us, and what are their likely consequences? There has been virtually no discussion of the option of adhering to the rule of law, as others do, for example Nicaragua, which I just mentioned (failing, of course, but no one will bar such moves by the U.S.) or as England did in the case of the IRA, or as the U.S. did when it was found that the Oklahoma City bombing was domestic in origin. And innumerable other cases.

Rather, there has, so far, been a solid drumbeat of calls for violent reaction, with only scarce mention of the fact that this will not only visit a terrible cost on wholly innocent victims, many of them Afghan victims of the Taliban, but also that it will answer the most fervent prayers of bin Laden and his network.

The second question is: "why?" This question is rarely raised in any serious way.

To refuse to face this question is to choose to increase significantly the probability of further crimes of this kind. There have been some exceptions. As I mentioned earlier, the *Wall Street Journal*, to its credit, reviewed the opinions of "moneyed Muslims," people who are pro-American but severely critical of U.S. policies in the region, for reasons that are familiar to anyone who has paid any attention. The feelings in the streets are similar, though far more bitter and angry.

The bin Laden network itself falls into a different category, and in fact its actions for 20 years have caused great harm to the poor and oppressed people of the region, who are not the concern of the terrorist networks. But they do draw from a reservoir of anger, fear, and desperation, which is why they are praying for a violent U.S. reaction, which will mobilize others to their horrendous cause.

Such topics as these should occupy the front pages—at least, if we hope to reduce the cycle of violence rather than to escalate it.

)

3.

The Ideological Campaign

Based on separate interviews with Radio B92 (Belgrade) on
September 18, 2001, Elise Fried and Peter Kreysler for DeutschlandFunk
Radio (Germany) on September 20, 2001, and Paola Leoni for *Giornale del
Popolo* (Switzerland) on September 21, 2001.

*Q: How do you see the media coverage of this event? Is there a
parallel to the Gulf War in "manufacturing consent"?*

CHOMSKY: Media coverage is not quite as uniform as
Europeans seem to believe, perhaps because they are keeping to the *New York Times*, National Public Radio, TV, and
so on. Even the *New York Times* conceded, this morning,
that attitudes in New York are quite unlike those they have
been conveying. It's a good story, also hinting at the fact
that the mainstream media have not been reporting this,
which is not entirely true, though it has been true, pretty
much, of the *New York Times*.

The *Times* now reports that "the drumbeat for war . . .
is barely audible on the streets of New York," and that calls
for peace "far outnumber demands for retribution," even
at the main "outdoor memorial to loss and grief" for the
victims of the atrocity. In fact, that's not unusual around
the country. There is surely virtually unanimous sentiment,

which all of us share, for apprehending and punishing the perpetrators, if they can be found. But I think there is probably strong majority sentiment against lashing out blindly and killing plenty of innocent people.

But it is entirely typical for the major media, and the intellectual classes generally, to line up in support of power at a time of crisis and try to mobilize the population for the same cause. That was true, with almost hysterical intensity, at the time of the bombing of Serbia. The Gulf War was not at all unusual.

And the pattern goes far back in history.

Assuming that the terrorists chose the World Trade Center as a symbolic target, how does globalization and cultural hegemony help create hatred towards America?

This is an extremely convenient belief for Western intellectuals. It absolves them of responsibility for the actions that actually do lie behind the choice of the World Trade Center. Was it bombed in 1993 because of concern over globalization and cultural hegemony? Was Sadat assassinated 20 years ago because of globalization? Is that why the "Afghanis" of the CIA-backed forces fought Russia in Afghanistan, or in Chechnya now?

A few days ago the *Wall Street Journal* reported attitudes of rich and privileged Egyptians who were at a McDonald's restaurant wearing stylish American clothes, etc., and who were bitterly critical of the U.S. for objective reasons of policy, which are well-known to those who wish to know: they had a report a few days earlier on attitudes of wealthy and privileged people in the region, all pro-American, and harshly critical of U.S. policies. Is that concern over "globalization," McDonald's, and jeans? Attitudes in the street are similar, but far more intense, and have nothing at all to do with these fashionable excuses.

These excuses are convenient for the U.S. and much of the West. To quote the lead analysis in the *New York Times* (September 16): "the perpetrators acted out of hatred for the values cherished in the West as freedom, tolerance, prosperity, religious pluralism and universal suffrage." U.S. actions are irrelevant, and therefore need not even be mentioned (Serge Schmemann). This is a comforting picture, and the general stance is not unfamiliar in intellectual history; in fact, it is close to the norm. It happens to be completely at variance with everything we know, but has all the merits of self-adulation and uncritical support for power. And it has the flaw that adopting it contributes significantly to the likelihood of further atrocities, including atrocities directed against us, perhaps even more horrendous ones than those of 9-11.

As for the bin Laden network, they have as little concern for globalization and cultural hegemony as they do for the poor and oppressed people of the Middle East who they have been severely harming for years. They tell us what their concerns are loud and clear: they are fighting a Holy War against the corrupt, repressive, and "un-Islamist" regimes of the region, and their supporters, just as they fought a Holy War against the Russians in the 1980s (and are now doing in Chechnya, western China,

Egypt—in this case since 1981, when they assassinated
Sadat—and elsewhere).

Bin Laden himself has probably never even heard of
"globalization." Those who have interviewed him in depth,
like Robert Fisk, report that he knows virtually nothing of
the world and doesn't care to. We can choose to ignore all
the facts and wallow in self-indulgent fantasies if we like,
but at considerable risk to ourselves, among others.
Among other things, we can also ignore, if we choose, the
roots of the "Afghanis" such as bin Laden and his associates, also not a secret.

*Are the American people educated to see this? Is there an
awareness of cause and effect?*

Unfortunately not, just as European people are not. What
is crucially important to privileged elements in the Middle East region (and even more so on the streets) is
scarcely understood here, particularly the most striking
example: the contrasting U.S. policies toward Iraq and
Israel's military occupation.

In Iraq, though Westerners prefer a different story, they
see that U.S. policy in the past ten years has devastated the
civilian society while strengthening Saddam Hussein—
who, as they know, the U.S. strongly supported through
his worst atrocities, including the gassing of the Kurds in
1988. When bin Laden makes these points in the broadcasts heard throughout the region, his audience
understands, even those who despise him, as many do.
About the U.S. and Israel, the most important facts are

scarcely even reported and are almost universally unknown, to elite intellectuals in particular.

People of the region do not, of course, share the comforting illusions prevalent in the U.S. about the "generous" and "magnanimous" offers at Camp David in summer 2000, let alone other favored myths.

There is extensive material in print on this, well documented from uncontroversial sources, but it is scarcely known.

How do you see the reaction of the American government? Whose will are they representing?

The United States government, like others, primarily responds to centers of concentrated domestic power. That should be a truism. Of course, there are other influences, including popular currents—that is true of all societies, even brutal totalitarian systems, and surely more democratic ones. Insofar as we have information, the U.S. government is now trying to exploit the opportunity to ram through its own agenda: militarization, including "missile defense," code words for the militarization of space; undermining social democratic programs; also undermining concerns over the harsh effects of corporate "globalization," or environmental issues, or health insurance, and so on; instituting measures that will intensify the transfer of wealth to the very few (for example, eliminating corporate taxes); and regimenting the society, so as to eliminate public debate and protest. All normal, and entirely natural. As for a response, they are, I presume, listening to foreign leaders, specialists on the Middle East, and I suppose their own intelligence agencies, who are warning them that a massive military response will answer bin Laden's prayers. But there are hawkish elements who want to use the occasion to strike out at their enemies, with extreme violence, no matter how many innocent people suffer, including people here and in Europe who will be victims of the escalating cycle of violence. All again in a very familiar dynamic. There are plenty of bin Ladens on both sides, as usual.

Economic globalization has spread the Western model all over the world, and the U.S.A. has been its prime supporter, sometimes with questionable means, often humiliating local cultures. Are we facing the consequences of the last decades of American strategic policy? Is America an innocent victim?

This thesis is commonly advanced. I don't agree. One reason is that the Western model—notably, the U.S. model—is based on vast state intervention into the economy. The "neoliberal rules" are like those of earlier eras. They are double-edged: market discipline is good for you, but not for me, except for temporary advantage, when I am in a good position to win the competition.

Secondly, what happened on September 11 has virtually nothing to do with economic globalization, in my opinion. The reasons lie elsewhere. Nothing can justify crimes such as those of September 11, but we can think of the United States as an "innocent victim" only if we adopt the convenient path of ignoring the record of its actions and those of its allies, which are, after all, hardly a secret.

Everybody agrees that nothing will be the same after 9-11, from a restriction of rights in daily life up to global strategy with new alliances and new enemies. What is your opinion about this?

[*Editor's note: Chomsky's response to this question, edited here, began by reiterating a point made in an earlier interview that September 11 was the first time since the War of 1812 that the national territory of the U.S. was attacked by foreign forces. See page 43.*]

I do not think it will lead to a long-term restriction of rights internally in any serious sense. The cultural and institutional barriers to that are too firmly rooted, I believe. If the U.S. chooses to respond by escalating the cycle of violence, which is most likely what bin Laden and his associates hope for, then the consequences could be awesome. There are, of course, other ways, lawful and constructive ones. And there are ample precedents for them. An aroused public within the more free and democratic societies can direct policies towards a much more humane and honorable course.

Worldwide intelligence services and the international systems of control (Echelon, for example) could not foresee what was going to happen, even if the international Islamic terrorism network was not unknown. How is it possible that the Big Brother's eyes were shut? Do we have to fear, now, a Bigger Big Brother?

I frankly have never been overly impressed with concerns widely voiced in Europe over Echelon as a system of control. As for worldwide intelligence systems, their failures over the years have been colossal, a matter I and others have written about and that I cannot pursue here.

That is true even when the targets of concern are far easier to deal with than the bin Laden network, which is no doubt so decentralized, so lacking in hierarchical structure, and so dispersed throughout much of the world as to have become largely impenetrable. The intelligence services will no doubt be given resources to try harder. But a serious effort to reduce the threat of this kind of terrorism, as in innumerable other cases, requires an effort to understand and to address the causes.

Bin Laden, the devil: is this an enemy or rather a brand, a sort of logo which identifies and personalizes the evil?

Bin Laden may or may not be directly implicated in these acts, but it is likely that the network in which he was a prime figure is—that is, the forces established by the United States and its allies for their own purposes and supported as long as they served those purposes. It is much easier to personalize the enemy, identified as the symbol of ultimate evil, than to seek to understand what lies behind major atrocities. And there are, naturally, very strong temptations to ignore one's own role—which in this case, is not difficult to unearth, and indeed is familiar to everyone who has any knowledge of the region and its recent history.

Doesn't this war risk becoming a new Vietnam? That trauma is still alive.

That is an analogy that is often raised. It reveals, in my opinion, the profound impact of several hundred years of imperial violence on the intellectual and moral culture of the West. The war in Vietnam began as a U.S. attack against South Vietnam, which was always the main target of the U.S. wars, and ended by devastating much of Indochina. Unless we are willing to face that elementary fact, we cannot talk seriously about the Vietnam war. It is true that the war proved costly to the U.S., though the impact on Indochina was incomparably more awful. The invasion of Afghanistan also proved costly to the U.S.S.R., but that is not the problem that comes to the fore when we consider that crime.

4.

Crimes of State

Based on excerpts from an interview with
David Barsamian on September 21, 2001.

Q: As you know, there is rage, anger and bewilderment in the U.S. since the September 11 events. There have been murders, attacks on mosques and even a Sikh temple. The University of Colorado, which is located here in Boulder, a town which has a liberal reputation, has graffiti saying, "Go home, Arabs," "Bomb Afghanistan," and "Go Home, Sand Niggers." What's your perspective on what has evolved since the terrorist attacks?

CHOMSKY: It's mixed. What you're describing certainly exists. On the other hand, countercurrents exist. I know they do where I have direct contacts, and hear the same from others.

[*Editor's note: Chomsky's response, edited here, echoes a comment he made in a previous interview in which he describes the mood in New York City and the emergence of a peace movement. See page 61.*]

That's another kind of current, also supportive of people who are being targeted here because they look dark or have a funny name. So there are countercurrents. The question is, what can we do to make the right ones prevail?

Do you think it's more than problematic to engage in alliances with individuals who are called "unsavory characters," drug traffickers and assassins, in order to achieve what is said to be a noble end?

Remember that some of the most unsavory characters are in the governments of the region, as well as in our own government, and the governments of our allies. If we're serious about it, we also have to ask, What is a noble end? Was it a noble end to draw the Russians into an "Afghan trap" in 1979, as Zbigniew Brzezinski claims he did? Supporting resistance against the Russian invasion in December 1979 is one thing. But inciting the invasion, as Brzezinski claims proudly that he did, and organizing a terrorist army of Islamic fanatics for your own purposes, is a different thing.

Another question we should be asking now is, What about the alliance that's being formed, that the U.S. is trying to put together? We should not forget that the U.S. itself is a leading terrorist state. What about the alliance between the U.S., Russia, China, Indonesia, Egypt, Algeria, all of whom are delighted to see an international system develop sponsored by the U.S. which will authorize them to carry out their own terrorist atrocities? Russia, for example, would be very happy to have U.S. backing for its murderous war in Chechnya. You have the same Afghanis fighting against Russia, also probably carrying out terrorist acts within Russia. As would perhaps India, in Kashmir. Indonesia would be delighted to have support for its massacres in Aceh. Algeria, as just announced on the broadcast we heard, would be delighted to have authorization to extend its own state terrorism. [*Editor's note: The broadcast Chomsky is referring to was the news report that aired immediately before his and Barsamian's live interview on KGNU (Boulder, Colorado).*] The same with China, fighting against separatist forces in its western provinces, including "Afghanis" who China and Iran had organized to fight the war against the Russians, beginning maybe as early as 1978, some reports indicate. And that runs through the world.

Not everyone will be admitted so easily into the coalition, however: we must, after all, maintain some standards. "The Bush administration warned [on October 6] that the leftist Sandinista party in Nicaragua, which hopes to return to power in elections next month, has maintained ties" with terrorist states and organizations, and therefore "cannot be counted on to support the international anti-terrorism coalition the administration has been attempting to forge" (George Gedda, AP, October 6). "As we stated previously there is no middle ground between those who oppose terrorism and those who support it," State Department spokeswoman Eliza Koch declared. Though the Sandinistas claim to have "abandoned the socialist policies and anti-American rhetoric of the past, Koch's statement [of October 6] indicated the administration has doubts about the claims of moderation." Washington's doubts are understandable. After all, Nicaragua had so outrageously attacked the U.S. that Ronald Reagan was compelled to declare a "national emergency" on May 1, 1985, renewed annually, because "the policies and actions of the Government of Nicaragua constitute an unusual and extraordinary threat to the national security and foreign policy of the United States." He also announced an embargo against Nicaragua "in response to the emergency situation created by the Nicaraguan Government's aggressive activities in Central America," namely its resistance to U.S. attack; the World Court dismissed as groundless Washington's claims of other activities. A year earlier, Reagan had designated May 1 as "Law Day," a celebration of our "200-year-old partnership between law and liberty," adding that without law there can be only "chaos and disorder." The day before, he celebrated Law Day by announcing that the United States would disregard the proceedings of the World Court, which went on to condemn his administration for its "unlawful use of force" and violation of treaties in its attack against Nicaragua, instantly escalated in response to the Court order to terminate the crime of international terrorism. Outside the U.S., of course, May 1 is a day of solidarity with the struggles of American workers.

It is, then, understandable that the U.S. should seek firm guarantees of good behavior before allowing a Sandinista-led Nicaragua to join the alliance of the just led by Washington, which is now welcoming others to join the war it has been waging against terrorism for 20 years: Russia, China, Indonesia, Turkey, and other worthy states, though of course not everyone.

Or, take the "Northern Alliance" that the U.S. and Russia are now jointly supporting. This is mostly a collection of warlords who carried out such destruction and terror that much of the population welcomed the Taliban. Furthermore, they are almost certainly involved in drug trafficking into Tajikistan. They control most of that border, and Tajikistan is reported to be a—maybe the—major transit point for the flow of drugs eventually to Europe and the United States. If the U.S. proceeds to join Russia in arming these forces heavily and launching some kind of offensive based on them, the drug flow is likely to increase under the ensuing conditions of chaos and refugee flight. The "unsavory characters" are, after all, familiar from a rich historical record, and the same is true of the "noble ends."

Your comment that the U.S. is a "leading terrorist state" might stun many Americans. Could you elaborate on that?

The most obvious example, though far from the most extreme case, is Nicaragua. It is the most obvious because it is uncontroversial, at least to people who have even the faintest concern for international law. [*Editor's note: See page 56 for Chomsky's more detailed elaboration on this point.*] It is worth remembering—particularly since it has been so uniformly suppressed—that the U.S. is the only country that was condemned for international terrorism by the World Court and that rejected a Security Council resolution calling on states to observe international law.

The United States continues international terrorism. There are also what in comparison are minor examples. Everybody here was quite properly outraged by the Okla-

homa City bombing, and for a couple of days the headlines read, "Oklahoma City Looks Like Beirut." I didn't
see anybody point out that Beirut also looks like Beirut,
and part of the reason is that the Reagan administration
had set off a terrorist bombing there in 1985 that was very
much like Oklahoma City, a truck bombing outside a
mosque timed to kill the maximum number of people as
they left. It killed 80 and wounded 250, mostly women and
children, according to a report in the *Washington Post* three
years later. The terrorist bombing was aimed at a Muslim
cleric whom they didn't like and whom they missed. It was
not very secret. I don't know what name you give to the
policies that are a leading factor in the death of maybe a
million civilians in Iraq and maybe a half a million children, which is the price the Secretary of State says we're
willing to pay. Is there a name for that? Supporting Israeli
atrocities is another one.

Supporting Turkey's crushing of its own Kurdish population, for which the Clinton administration gave the
decisive support, 80 percent of the arms, escalating as
atrocities increased, is another. And that was a truly massive atrocity, one of the worst campaigns of ethnic
cleansing and destruction in the 1990s, scarcely known
because of the primary U.S. responsibility—and when
impolitely brought up, dismissed as a minor "flaw" in our
general dedication to "ending inhumanity" everywhere.

Or take the destruction of the Al-Shifa pharmaceutical
plant in Sudan, one little footnote in the record of state
terror, quickly forgotten. What would the reaction have
been if the bin Laden network had blown up half the

pharmaceutical supplies in the U.S. and the facilities for replenishing them? We can imagine, though the comparison is unfair: the consequences are vastly more severe in Sudan. That aside, if the U.S. or Israel or England were to be the target of such an atrocity, what would the reaction be? In this case we say, "Oh, well, too bad, minor mistake, let's go on to the next topic, let the victims rot." Other people in the world don't react like that. When bin Laden brings up that bombing, he strikes a resonant chord, even among those who despise and fear him; and the same, unfortunately, is true of much of the rest of his rhetoric.

Though it is merely a footnote, the Sudan case is nonetheless highly instructive. One interesting aspect is the reaction when someone dares to mention it. I have in the past, and did so again in response to queries from journalists shortly after the 9-11 atrocities. I mentioned that the toll of the "horrendous crime" of 9-11, committed with "wickedness and awesome cruelty" (quoting Robert Fisk), may be comparable to the consequences of Clinton's bombing of the Al-Shifa plant in August 1998. That plausible conclusion elicited an extraordinary reaction, filling many web sites and journals with feverish and fanciful condemnations, which I'll ignore. The only important aspect is that that single sentence—which, on a closer look, appears to be an understatement—was regarded by some commentators as utterly scandalous. It is difficult to avoid the conclusion that at some deep level, however they may deny it to themselves, they regard our crimes against the weak to be as normal as the air we breathe. Our crimes, for which we are responsible: as taxpayers, for failing to provide massive reparations, for granting refuge and immunity to the perpetrators, and for allowing the terrible facts to be sunk deep in the memory hole. All of this is of great significance, as it has been in the past.

About the consequences of the destruction of the Al-Shifa plant, we have only estimates. Sudan sought a UN inquiry into the justifications for the bombing, but even that was blocked by Washington, and few seem to have tried to investigate beyond. But we surely should. Perhaps we should begin by recalling some virtual truisms, at least among those with a minimal concern for human rights. When we estimate the human toll of a crime, we count not only those who were literally murdered on the spot but those who died as a result. That is the course we adopt reflexively, and properly, when we consider the crimes of official enemies—Stalin, Hitler, and Mao, to mention the most extreme cases. Here, we do not consider the crime to be mitigated by the fact that it was not intended but was a reflection of institutional and ideological structures: the Chinese famine of 1958-1961, to take an extreme case, is not dismissed on grounds that it was a "mistake" and that Mao did not "intend" to kill tens of millions of people. Nor is it mitigated by speculations about his personal reasons for the orders that led to the famine. Similarly, we would dismiss with contempt the charge that condemnation of Hitler's crimes in Eastern Europe overlooks Stalin's crimes. If we are even pretending to be serious, we apply the same standards to ourselves, always. In this case, we count the number who died as a consequence of the crime, not just those killed in Khartoum by cruise missiles; and we do not consider the crime to be mitigated by the fact that it reflects the normal functioning of policymaking and ideological institutions—as it did, even if there is some validity to the (to my mind, dubious) speculations about Clinton's personal problems, which are irrelevant to this question anyway, for the reasons that everyone takes for granted when considering the crimes of official enemies.

With these truisms in mind, let's have a look at some of the material that was readily available in the mainstream press. I disregard the extensive analysis of the validity of Washington's pretexts, of little moral significance in comparison to the question of consequences.

A year after the attack, "without the lifesaving medicine [the destroyed facilities] produced, Sudan's death toll from the bombing has continued, quietly, to rise . . . Thus, tens of thousands of people—many of them children—have suffered and died from malaria, tuberculosis, and other treatable diseases . . . [Al-Shifa] provided affordable medicine for humans and all the locally available veterinary medicine in Sudan. It produced 90 percent of Sudan's major pharmaceutical products . . . Sanctions against Sudan make it impossible to import adequate amounts of medicines required to cover the serious gap left by the plant's destruction . . . [T]he action taken by Washington on August 20, 1998, continues to deprive the people of Sudan of needed medicine. Millions must wonder how the International Court of Justice in The Hague will celebrate this anniversary" (Jonathan Belke, *Boston Globe*, August 22, 1999).

Germany's Ambassador to Sudan writes that "It is difficult to assess how many people in this poor African country died as a consequence of the destruction of the Al-Shifa factory, but several tens of thousands seems a reasonable guess" (Werner Daum, "Universalism and the West," *Harvard International Review*, Summer 2001).

"[T]he loss of this factory is a tragedy for the rural communities who need these medicines" (Tom Carnaffin, technical manager with "intimate knowledge" of the destroyed plant, quoted in Ed Vulliamy, Henry McDonald, Shyam Bhatia, and Martin Bright, *London Observer*, August 23, 1998, lead story, page 1).

Al-Shifa "provided 50 percent of Sudan's medicines, and its destruction has left the country with no supplies of chloroquine, the standard treatment for malaria," but months later, the British Labour government refused requests "to resupply chloroquine in emergency relief until such time as the Sudanese can rebuild their pharmaceutical production" (Patrick Wintour, *Observer*, December 20, 1998).

The Al-Shifa facility was "the only one producing TB drugs—for more than 100,000 patients, at about 1 British pound a month. Costlier imported versions are not an option for most of them—or for their husbands, wives and children, who will have been infected since. Al-Shifa was also the only factory making veterinary drugs in this vast, mostly pastoralist, country. Its speciality was drugs to kill the parasites which pass from herds to herders, one of Sudan's principal causes of infant mortality" (James Astill, *Guardian*, October 2, 2001).

The silent death toll continues to mount.

These accounts are by respected journalists writing in

leading journals. The one exception is the most knowl-
edgeable of the sources just cited, Jonathan Belke, regional
program manager for the Near East Foundation, who
writes on the basis of field experience in Sudan. The Foundation is a respected development institution dating back
to World War I. It provides technical assistance to poor
countries in the Middle East and Africa, emphasizing
grassroots locally-run development projects, and operates
with close connections to major universities, charitable
organizations, and the State Department, including well-
known Middle East diplomats and prominent figures in
Middle East educational and developmental affairs.

According to credible analyses readily available to us,
then, proportional to population, the destruction of Al-
Shifa is as if the bin Laden network, in a single attack on
the U.S., caused "hundreds of thousands of people—many
of them children—to suffer and die from easily treatable
diseases," though the analogy, as noted, is unfair. Sudan is
"one of the least developed areas in the world. Its harsh cli-
mate, scattered populations, health hazards and crumbling
infrastructure combine to make life for many Sudanese a
struggle for survival"; a country with endemic malaria,
tuberculosis, and many other diseases, where "periodic out-
breaks of meningitis or cholera are not uncommon," so
affordable medicines are a dire necessity (Jonathan Belke
and Kamal El-Faki, technical reports from the field for the
Near East Foundation). It is, furthermore, a country with
limited arable land, a chronic shortage of potable water, a
huge death rate, little industry, an unserviceable debt,
wracked with AIDS, devastated by a vicious and destruc-

tive internal war, and under severe sanctions. What is happening within is largely speculation, including Belke's (quite plausible) estimate that within a year tens of thousands had already "suffered and died" as the result of the destruction of the major facilities for producing affordable drugs and veterinary medicines.

This only scratches the surface

Human Rights Watch immediately reported that as an immediate consequence of the bombing, "all UN agencies based in Khartoum have evacuated their American staff, as have many other relief organizations," so that "many relief efforts have been postponed indefinitely, including a crucial one run by the U.S.-based International Rescue Committee [in a government town] where more than fifty southerners are dying daily"; these are regions in "southern Sudan, where the UN estimates that 2.4 million people are at risk of starvation," and the "disruption in assistance" for the "devastated population" may produce a "terrible crisis."

What is more, the U.S. bombing "appears to have shattered the slowly evolving move toward compromise between Sudan's warring sides" and terminated promising steps towards a peace agreement to end the civil war that had left 1.5 million dead since 1981, which might have also led to "peace in Uganda and the entire Nile Basin." The attack apparently "shattered . . . the expected benefits of a political shift at the heart of Sudan's Islamist government" towards a "pragmatic engagement with the outside world," along with efforts to address Sudan's domestic crises, to end support for terrorism, and to reduce the influence of radical Islamists (Mark Huband, *Financial Times*, September 8, 1998).

Insofar as such consequences ensued, we may compare the crime in Sudan to the assassination of Lumumba, which helped plunge the Congo into decades of slaughter, still continuing; or the overthrow of the democratic government of Guatemala in 1954, which led to forty years of hideous atrocities; and all too many others like it.

Huband's conclusions are reiterated three years later by James Astill, in the article just cited. He reviews "the political cost to a country struggling to emerge from totalitarian military dictatorship, ruinous Islamism and long-running civil war" before the missile attack, which "overnight [plunged Khartoum] into the nightmare of impotent extremism it had been trying to escape." This "political cost" may have been even more harmful to Sudan than the destruction of its "fragile medical services," he concludes.

Astill quotes Dr. Idris Eltayeb, one of Sudan's handful of pharmacologists and chairman of the board of Al-Shifa: the crime, he says, is "just as much an act of terrorism as at the Twin Towers—the only difference is we know who did it. I feel very sad about the loss of life [in New York and Washington], but in terms of numbers, and the relative cost to a poor country, [the bombing in Sudan] was worse."

Unfortunately, he may be right about "the loss of life in terms of numbers," even if we do not take into account the longer-term "political cost."

Evaluating "relative cost" is an enterprise I won't try to pursue, and it goes without saying that ranking crimes on some scale is generally ridiculous, though comparison of the toll is perfectly reasonable and indeed standard in scholarship.

The bombing also carried severe costs for the people of the United States, as became glaringly evident on September 11, or should have. It seems to me remarkable that this has not been brought up prominently (if at all), in the extensive discussion of intelligence failures that lie behind the 9-11 atrocities.

Just before the 1998 missile strike, Sudan detained two men suspected of bombing the American embassies in East Africa, notifying Washington, U.S. officials confirmed. But the U.S. rejected Sudan's offer of cooperation, and after the missile attack, Sudan "angrily released" the suspects (James Risen, *New York Times*, July 30, 1999); they have since been identified as bin Laden operatives. Recently leaked FBI memos add another reason why Sudan "angrily released" the suspects. The memos reveal that the FBI wanted them extradited, but the State Department refused. One "senior CIA source" now describes this and other rejections of Sudanese offers of cooperation as "the worst single intelligence failure in this whole terrible business" of September 11. "It is the key to the whole thing right now" because of the voluminous evidence on bin Laden that Sudan offered to produce, offers that were repeatedly rebuffed because of the administration's "irrational hatred" of Sudan, the senior CIA source reports. Included in Sudan's rejected offers was "a vast intelligence database on Osama bin Laden and more than 200 leading members of his al-Qaeda terrorist network in the years leading up to the 11 September attacks." Washington was "offered thick files, with photographs and detailed biographies of many of his principal cadres, and vital information about al-Qaeda's financial interests in many parts of the globe," but refused to accept the information, out of "irrational hatred" of the target of its missile attack. "It is reasonable to say that had we had this data we may have had a better chance of preventing the attacks" of September 11, the same senior CIA source concludes (David Rose, *Observer*, September 30, reporting an *Observer* investigation).

One can scarcely try to estimate the toll of the Sudan bombing, even apart from the probable tens of thousands of immediate Sudanese victims. The complete toll is attributable to the single act of terror—at least, if we have the honesty to adopt the standards we properly apply to official enemies. The reaction in the West tells us a lot about ourselves, if we agree to adopt another moral truism: look into the mirror.

Or to return to "our little region over here which never has bothered anybody," as Henry Stimson called the Western hemisphere, take Cuba. After many years of terror beginning in late 1959, including very serious atrocities, Cuba should have the right to resort to violence against the U.S. according to U.S. doctrine that is scarcely questioned. It is, unfortunately, all too easy to continue, not only with regard to the U.S. but also other terrorist states.

In your book Culture of Terrorism, *you write that "the cultural scene is illuminated with particular clarity by the thinking of the liberal doves, who set the limits for respectable dissent." How have they been performing since the events of September 11?*

Since I don't like to generalize, let's take a concrete example. On September 16, the *New York Times* reported that the U.S. has demanded that Pakistan cut off food aid to Afghanistan. That had already been hinted before, but here it was stated flat out. Among other demands Washington issued to Pakistan, it also "demanded . . . the elimination of truck convoys that provide much of the food and other supplies to Afghanistan's civilian population"—the food that is keeping probably millions of people just this side of starvation (John Burns, Islamabad, *New York Times*). What does that mean? That means that unknown numbers of starving Afghans will die. Are these Taliban? No, they're victims of the Taliban. Many of them are internal refugees kept from leaving. But here's a statement saying, OK, let's proceed to kill unknown numbers, maybe millions, of starving Afghans who are victims of the Taliban. What was the reaction?

I spent almost the entire day afterwards on radio and television around the world. I kept bringing it up. Nobody in Europe or the U.S. could think of one word of reaction. Elsewhere in the world there was plenty of reaction, even around the periphery of Europe, like Greece. How should we have reacted to this? Suppose some power was strong enough to say, Let's do something that will cause a huge number of Americans to die of starvation. Would you think it's a serious problem? And again, it's not a fair analogy. In the case of Afghanistan, left to rot after it had been ruined by the Soviet invasion and exploited for Washington's war, much of the country is in ruins and its people are desperate, already one of the worst humanitarian crises in the world.

National Public Radio, which in the 1980s was denounced by the Reagan administration as "Radio Managua on the Potomac," is also considered "out there" on the liberal end of respectable debate. Noah Adams, the host of All Things Considered, *asked these questions on September 17: "Should assassinations be allowed? Should the CIA be given more operating leeway?"*

The CIA should not be permitted to carry out assassinations, but that's the least of it. Should the CIA be permitted to organize a car bombing in Beirut like the one I just mentioned?

Not a secret, incidentally; prominently reported in the mainstream, though easily forgotten. That didn't violate any laws. And it's not just the CIA. Should they have been permitted to organize in Nicaragua a terrorist army that had the official task, straight out of the mouth of the State Department, to attack "soft targets" in Nicaragua, meaning undefended agricultural cooperatives and health clinics? Remember that the State Department officially approved such attacks immediately after the World Court had ordered the U.S. to end its international terrorist campaign and pay substantial reparations.

What's the name for that? Or to set up something like

the bin Laden network, not him himself, but the background organizations?

Should the U.S. be authorized to provide Israel with attack helicopters used to carry out political assassinations and attacks on civilian targets? That's not the CIA. That's the Clinton administration, with no noticeable objection. In fact, it wasn't even reported, though the sources were impeccable.

Could you very briefly define the political uses of terrorism? Where does it fit in the doctrinal system?

The U.S. is officially committed to what is called "low-intensity warfare." That's the official doctrine. If you read the standard definitions of low-intensity conflict and compare them with official definitions of "terrorism" in army manuals, or the U.S. Code (see p. 47, footnote), you find they're almost the same. Terrorism is the use of coercive means aimed at civilian populations in an effort to achieve political, religious, or other aims. That's what the World Trade Center attack was, a particularly horrifying terrorist crime.

Terrorism, according to the official definitions, is simply part of state action, official doctrine, and not just that of the U.S., of course.

It is not, as is often claimed, "the weapon of the weak."

Furthermore, all of these things should be well known. It's shameful that they're not. Anybody who wants to find out about them can begin by reading the Alex George collection mentioned earlier, which runs through lots and lots of cases. These are things people need to know if they want to understand anything about themselves. They are known by the victims, of course, but the perpetrators prefer to look elsewhere.

5.

Choice of Action

Based on an interview with Michael Albert on September 22, 2001.

Q: Let's assume, for the sake of discussion, that bin Laden was behind the events. If so, what reason might he have had? It certainly can't help poor and disempowered people anywhere, much less Palestinians, so what is his aim, if he planned the action?

CHOMSKY: One has to be cautious about this. According to Robert Fisk, who has interviewed him repeatedly and at length, Osama bin Laden shares the anger felt throughout the region at the U.S. military presence in Saudi Arabia, support for atrocities against Palestinians, along with U.S.-led devastation of Iraqi civilian society. That feeling of anger is shared by rich and poor, and across the political and other spectrums.

Many who know the conditions well are also dubious about bin Laden's capacity to plan that incredibly sophisticated operation from a cave somewhere in Afghanistan. But that his network was involved is highly plausible, and that he is an inspiration for them, also. These are decentralized, non-hierarchic structures, probably with quite limited communication links among them. It's entirely possible that bin Laden's telling the truth when he says he didn't know about the operation.

All that aside, bin Laden is quite clear about what he wants, not only to any westerners who want to interview him, like Fisk, but more importantly to the Arabic-speaking audience that he reaches through the cassettes that circulate widely. Adopting his framework for the sake of discussion, the prime target is Saudi Arabia and other corrupt and repressive regimes of the region, none of which are truly "Islamic." And he and his network are intent on supporting Muslims defending themselves against "infidels" wherever it may be: Chechnya, Bosnia, Kashmir, Western China, Southeast Asia, North Africa, maybe elsewhere. They fought and won a Holy War to drive the Russians (Europeans who are presumably not relevantly different from British or Americans in their view) out of Muslim Afghanistan, and they are even more intent on driving the Americans out of Saudi Arabia, a far more important country to them, as it is the home of the holiest Islamic sites.

His call for the overthrow of corrupt and brutal regimes of gangsters and torturers resonates quite widely, as does his indignation against the atrocities that he and others attribute to the United States, hardly without reason. It's entirely true that his crimes are extremely harmful to the poorest and most oppressed people of the region. The latest attacks, for example, were extremely harmful to the Palestinians. But what looks like sharp inconsistency from outside may be perceived rather differently from within. By courageously fighting oppressors, who are quite real, bin Laden may appear to be a hero, however harmful his actions are to the poor majority. And if the United States succeeds in killing him, he may become even more powerful as a martyr whose voice will continue to be heard on the cassettes that are circulating and through other means. He is, after all, as much of a symbol as an objective force, both for the U.S. and probably much of the population.

There's every reason, I think, to take him at his word. And his crimes can hardly come as a surprise to the CIA. "Blowback" from the radical Islamic forces organized, armed, and trained by the U.S., Egypt, France, Pakistan, and others began almost at once, with the 1981 assassination of President Sadat of Egypt, one of the most enthusiastic of the creators of the forces assembled to fight a Holy War against the Russians. The violence has been continuing since without letup.

The blowback has been quite direct, and of a kind very familiar from fifty years of history, including the drug flow and the violence. To take one case, the leading specialist on this topic, John Cooley, reports that CIA officers "consciously assisted" the entry of the radical Islamic Egyptian cleric Sheikh Omar Abdel Rahman to the U.S. in 1990 (*Unholy Wars*). He was already wanted by Egypt on charges of terrorism. In 1993, he was implicated in the bombing of the World Trade Center, which followed procedures taught in CIA manuals that were, presumably, provided to the "Afghanis" fighting the Russians. The plan was to blow up the UN building, the Lincoln and Holland tunnels, and other targets as well. Sheikh Omar was convicted of conspiracy and given a long jail sentence.

Again, if bin Laden planned these actions, and especially if popular fears of more such actions to come are credible, what is the proper approach to reducing or eliminating the danger? What steps should be taken by the U.S. or others, domestically or internationally? What would be the results of those steps?

Every case is different, but let's take a few analogies. What was the right way for Britain to deal with IRA bombs in London? One choice would have been to send the RAF to bomb the source of their finances, places like Boston, or to infiltrate commandos to capture those suspected of involvement in such financing and kill them or spirit them to London to face trial.

Putting aside feasibility, that would have been criminal idiocy. Another possibility was to consider realistically the background concerns and grievances, and to try to remedy them, while at the same time following the rule of law to punish criminals. That would make a lot more sense, one would think. Or take the bombing of the federal building in Oklahoma City. There were immediate calls for bombing the Middle East, and it probably would have happened if even a remote hint of a link had been found. When it was instead discovered to be a domestically devised attack, by someone with militia connections, there was no call to obliterate Montana and Idaho, or the "Republic of Texas," which has been calling for secession from the oppressive and illegitimate government in Washington. Rather, there was a search for the perpetrator, who was found, brought to court, and sentenced, and to the extent that the reaction was sensible, there were efforts to understand the grievances that lie behind such crimes and to address the problems. At least, that is the course we follow if we have any concern for genuine justice and hope to reduce the likelihood of further atrocities rather than increase it. The same principles hold quite generally, with due attention to variation of circumstances. Specifically, they hold in this case.

What steps, in contrast, is the U.S. government seeking to undertake? What will be the results, if they succeed in their plans?

What has been announced is a virtual declaration of war against all who do not join Washington in its resort to violence, however it chooses.

The nations of the world face a "stark choice": join us in our crusade or "face the certain prospect of death and destruction" (R. W. Apple, *New York Times*, September 14). Bush's rhetoric of September 20 forcefully reiterates that stance. Taken literally, it's virtually a declaration of war against much of the world. But I am sure we should not take it literally. Government planners do not want to undermine their own interests so grievously. What their actual plans are, we do not know. But I suppose they will take to heart the warnings they are receiving from foreign leaders, specialists in the region, and presumably their own intelligence agencies that a massive military assault, which would kill many innocent civilians, would be exactly "what the perpetrators of the Manhattan slaughter must want above all. Military retaliation would elevate their cause, idolize their leader, devalue moderation and validate fanaticism. If ever history needed a catalyst for a new and awful conflict between Arabs and the West, this could be it" (Simon Jenkins, *Times* [London], September 14, one of many who made these points insistently from the outset).

Even if bin Laden is killed—maybe even more so if he is killed—a slaughter of innocents would only intensify the feelings of anger, desperation and frustration that are rampant in the region, and mobilize others to his horrendous cause.

What the administration does will depend, in part at least, on the mood at home, which we can hope to influence. What the consequences of their actions will be we cannot say with much confidence, any more than they can. But there are plausible estimates, and unless the course of reason, law, and treaty obligations is pursued, the prospects could be quite grim.

Many people say that the citizens of Arab nations should have taken responsibility to remove terrorists from the planet, or governments that support terrorists. How do you react?

It makes sense to call upon citizens to eliminate terrorists instead of electing them to high office, lauding and rewarding them. But I would not suggest that we should have "removed our elected officials, their advisers, their intellectual claque, and their clients from the planet," or destroyed our own and other Western governments because of their terrorist crimes and their support for terrorists worldwide, including many who were transferred from favored friends and allies to the category of "terrorists" because they disobeyed U.S. orders: Saddam Hussein, and many others like him. However, it is rather unfair to blame citizens of harsh and brutal regimes that we support for not undertaking this responsibility, when we do not do so under vastly more propitious circumstances.

Many people say that all through history when a nation is attacked, it attacks in kind. How do you react?

When countries are attacked they try to defend themselves, if they can. According to the doctrine proposed, Nicaragua, South Vietnam, Cuba, and numerous others should have been setting off bombs in Washington and other U.S. cities, Palestinians should be applauded for bombings in Tel Aviv, and on and on. It is because such doctrines had brought Europe to virtual self-annihilation after hundreds of years of savagery that the nations of the world forged a different compact after World War II, establishing—at least formally—the principle that the resort to force is barred except in the case of self-defense against armed attack until the Security Council acts to protect international peace and security. Specifically, retaliation is barred. Since the U.S. is not under armed attack, in the sense of Article 51 of the UN Charter, these considerations are irrelevant—at least, if we agree that the fundamental principles of international law should apply to ourselves, not only to those we dislike.

International law aside, we have centuries of experience that tell us exactly what is entailed by the doctrines now being proposed and hailed by many commentators. In a world with weapons of mass destruction, what it entails is an imminent termination of the human experiment—which is, after all, why Europeans decided half a century ago that the game of mutual slaughter in which they had been indulging for centuries had better come to an end, or else.

In the immediate aftermath of 9-11, many people were horrified to see expressions of anger at the U.S. emanating from various parts of the world, including but not confined to the Middle East. Images of people celebrating the destruction of the World Trade Center leave people wanting revenge. How do you react to that?

A U.S.-backed army took control in Indonesia in 1965, organizing the slaughter of hundreds of thousands of people, mostly landless peasants, in a massacre that the CIA compared to the crimes of Hitler, Stalin, and Mao. The massacre, accurately reported, elicited uncontrolled euphoria in the West, in the national media and elsewhere. Indonesian peasants had not harmed us in any way. When Nicaragua finally succumbed to the U.S. assault, the mainstream press lauded the success of the methods adopted to "wreck the economy and prosecute a long and deadly proxy war until the exhausted natives overthrow the unwanted government themselves," with a cost to us that is "minimal," leaving the victims "with wrecked bridges, sabotaged power stations, and ruined farms," and thus providing the U.S. candidate with "a winning issue": ending the "impoverishment of the people of Nicaragua" (*Time*).

We are "United in Joy" at this outcome, the *New York Times* proclaimed. It's easy to continue.

Very few people around the world celebrated the crimes in New York; overwhelmingly, the atrocities were passionately deplored, even in places where people have been ground underfoot by Washington's boots for a long, long time. But there were undoubtedly feelings of anger at the United States. However, I am aware of nothing as grotesque as the two examples I just mentioned, or many more like them in the West.

Getting beyond these public reactions, in your view what are the actual motivations operating in U.S. policy at this moment? What is the purpose of the "war on terror," as proposed by Bush?

The "war on terror" is neither new nor a "war on terror." We should recall that the Reagan administration came to office 20 years ago proclaiming that "international terrorism" (sponsored worldwide by the Soviet Union) is the greatest threat faced by the U.S., which is the main target of terrorism, and its allies and friends. We must therefore dedicate ourselves to a war to eradicate this "cancer," this "plague" that is destroying civilization. The Reaganites acted on that commitment by organizing campaigns of international terrorism that were extraordinary in scale and destruction, even leading to a World Court condemnation of the U.S., while lending their support to innumerable others, for example, in southern Africa, where Western-backed South African depredations killed a million and a half people and caused $60 billion of damage during the Reagan years alone. Hysteria over international terrorism peaked in the mid-80s, while the U.S. and its allies were well in the lead in spreading the cancer they were demanding must be extirpated.

If we choose, we can live in a world of comforting illusion. Or we can look at recent history, at the institutional structures that remain essentially unchanged, at the plans that are being announced—and answer the questions accordingly. I know of no reason to suppose that there has been a sudden change in long-standing motivations or policy goals, apart from tactical adjustments to changing circumstances.

We should also remember that one exalted task of intellectuals is to proclaim every few years that we have "changed course," the past is behind us and can be forgotten as we march on towards a glorious future. That is a highly convenient stance, though hardly an admirable or sensible one.

The literature on all this is voluminous. There is no reason, beyond choice, to remain unaware of the facts—which are, of course, familiar to the victims, though few of them are in a position to recognize the scale or nature of the international terrorist assault to which they are subjected.

Do you believe that most Americans will, as conditions permit more detailed evaluation of options, accept that the solution to terror attacks on civilians here is for the U.S. to respond with terror attacks against civilians abroad, and that the solution to fanaticism is surveillance and curtailed civil liberties?

I hope not, but we should not underestimate the capacity of well-run propaganda systems to drive people to irrational, murderous, and suicidal behavior. Take an example that is remote enough so that we should be able to look at it with some dispassion: World War I. It can't have been that both sides were engaged in a noble war for the highest objectives. But on both sides, the soldiers marched off to mutual slaughter with enormous exuberance, fortified by the cheers of the intellectual classes and those who they helped mobilize, across the political spectrum, from left to right, including the most powerful left political force in the world, in Germany. Exceptions are so few that we can practically list them, and some of the most prominent among them ended up in jail for questioning the nobility of the enterprise: among them Rosa Luxemburg, Bertrand Russell, and Eugene Debs. With the help of Wilson's propaganda agencies and the enthusiastic support of liberal intellectuals, a pacifist country was turned in a few months into raving anti-German hysterics, ready to take revenge on those who had perpetrated savage crimes, many of them invented by the British Ministry of Information. But that's by no means inevitable, and we should not underestimate the civilizing effects of the popular struggles of recent years. We need not stride resolutely towards catastrophe, merely because those are the marching orders.

6.

Civilizations East and West

Based on interviews with European media September 20-22, 2001 with Marili Margomenou for Alpha TV Station (Greece), Miguel Mora for *El País* (Spain), Natalie Levisalles for *Liberation* (France).

[*Editor's note: As many of these questions were written by journalists who speak English as a second language, in some instances phrases were edited for clarity with every effort to preserve the intended meaning.*]

Q: After the attack in the U.S.A., Secretary of State Colin L. Powell said that the U.S. government will revise the laws for terrorism, including the law of 1976 that prohibits assassinations of foreigners. The European Union is also about to apply a new law on terrorism. How might response to the attacks come to constrict our freedoms? For instance, does terrorism give government the right to put us under surveillance, in order to trace suspects and prevent future attacks?

CHOMSKY: A response that is too abstract may be misleading, so let us consider a current and quite typical illustration of what plans to relax constraints on state violence mean in practice. This morning (September 21), the *New York Times* ran an opinion piece by Michael Walzer, a respected intellectual who is considered a moral leader. He called for an "ideological campaign to engage all the arguments and excuses for terrorism and reject them"; since, as he knows, there are no such arguments and excuses for terrorism of the kind he has in mind, at least on the part of anyone amenable to reason, in effect this translates as a call to reject efforts to explore the reasons that lie behind terrorist acts that are directed against states he supports. He then proceeds, in conventional fashion, to enlist himself among those who provide "arguments and excuses for terrorism," tacitly endorsing political assassination, namely, Israeli assassinations of Palestinians who Israel claims support terrorism; no evidence is offered or considered necessary, and in many cases even the suspicions appear groundless. And the inevitable "collateral damage"— women, children, others nearby—is treated in the standard way. U.S.-supplied attack helicopters have been used for such assassinations for ten months.

Walzer puts the word "assassination" in quotes, indicating that in his view, the term is part of what he calls the "fervid and highly distorted accounts of the blockade of Iraq and the Israeli-Palestinian conflict." He is referring to criticism of U.S.-backed Israeli atrocities in the territories that have been under harsh and brutal military occupation for almost thirty-five years, and of U.S. policies that have devastated the civilian society of Iraq (while strengthening Saddam Hussein). Such criticisms are marginal in the U.S., but too much for him, apparently. By "distorted accounts," perhaps Walzer has in mind occasional references to the statement of Secretary of State Madeleine Albright over national TV when she was asked about the estimates of a half million deaths of Iraqi children as a result of the sanctions regime. She recognized that such consequences were a "hard choice" for her administration, but said "we think the price is worth it."

I mention this single example, easily multiplied, to illustrate the substantive meaning of the relaxation of constraints on state action. We may recall that violent and murderous states quite commonly justify their actions as "counter-terrorism": for example, the Nazis fighting partisan resistance. And such actions are commonly justified by respected intellectuals.

That is not ancient history. In December 1987, at the peak of concern over international terrorism, the UN General Assembly passed its major resolution on the matter, condemning the plague in the strongest terms and calling on all nations to act forcefully to overcome it. The resolution passed 153-2 (U.S. and Israel), Honduras alone abstaining. The offending passage states "that nothing in the present resolution could in any way prejudice the right to self-determination, freedom and independence, as derived from the Charter of the United Nations, of peoples forcibly deprived of that right . . . , particularly peoples under colonial and racist regimes and foreign occupation or other forms of colonial domination, nor . . . the right of these peoples to struggle to this end and to seek and receive support [in accordance with the Charter and other principles of international law]." These rights are not accepted by the U.S. and Israel; or at the time, their South African ally. For Washington, the African National Congress was a "terrorist organization," but South Africa did not join Cuba and others as a "terrorist state." Washington's interpretation of "terrorism" of course prevails, in practice, with human consequences that have been severe.

There is now much talk about formulating a Comprehensive Convention against Terrorism, no small task. The reason, carefully skirted in reports, is that the U.S. will not accept anything like the offending passage of the 1987 resolution, and none of its allies will accept it either if the definition of "terrorism" conforms to official definitions in the U.S. Code or army manuals, but only if it can somehow be reshaped to exclude the terrorism of the powerful and their clients.

To be sure, there are many factors to be considered in thinking about your question. But the historical record is of overwhelming importance. At a very general level, the question cannot be answered. It depends on specific circumstances and specific proposals.

Bundestag in Germany already decided that German soldiers will join American forces, although 80 percent of the German people do not agree with this, according to a survey of the Forsa Institute. What are your thoughts on this?

For the moment, European powers are hesitant about joining Washington's crusade, fearing that by a massive assault against innocent civilians the U.S. will provide bin Laden, or others like him, with a way to mobilize desperate and angry people to their cause, with consequences that could be even more horrifying.

What do you think about nations acting as a global community during a time of war? It is not the first time that every country must ally with the U.S.A., or be considered an enemy, but now Afghanistan is declaring the same thing.

The Bush administration at once presented the nations of the world with a choice: join us, or face destruction. [*Editor's note: Here Chomsky is referring to a quote published in the* New York Times, *September 14, 2001. See page 64.*]

The "global community" strongly opposes terror, including the massive terror of the powerful states, and also the terrible crimes of September 11. But the "global community" does not act. When Western states and intellectuals use the term "international community," they are referring to themselves. For example, NATO bombing of Serbia was undertaken by the "international community" according to consistent Western rhetoric, although those who did not have their heads buried in the sand knew that it was opposed by most of the world, often quite vocally. Those who do not support the actions of wealth and power are not part of "the global community," just as "terrorism" conventionally means "terrorism directed against us and our friends."

It is hardly surprising that Afghanistan is attempting to mimic the U.S., calling on Muslims for support. The scale, of course, is vastly smaller. Even as remote as they are from the world outside, Taliban leaders presumably know full well that the Islamic states are not their friends. These states have, in fact, been subjected to terrorist attack by the radical Islamist forces that were organized and trained to fight a Holy War against the U.S.S.R. twenty years ago, and began to pursue their own terrorist agenda elsewhere immediately, with the assassination of Egyptian president Sadat.

According to you, an attack against Afghanistan is a "war against terrorism"?

An attack against Afghanistan will probably kill a great many innocent civilians, possibly enormous numbers in a country where millions are already on the verge of death from starvation. Wanton killing of innocent civilians is terrorism, not a war against terrorism.

Could you imagine how the situation would be if the terrorist's attack in the U.S.A. had happened during the night, when very few people would be in the WTC? In other words, if there were very few victims, would the American government react in the same way? Up to what point is it influenced by the symbolism of this disaster, the fact that it was the Pentagon and the Twin Towers that were hit?

I doubt that it would have made any difference. It would have been a terrible crime even if the toll had been much smaller. The Pentagon is more than a "symbol," for reasons that need no comment. As for the World Trade Center, we scarcely know what the terrorists had in mind when they bombed it in 1993 and destroyed it on September 11. But we can be quite confident that it had little to do with such matters as "globalization," or "economic imperialism," or "cultural values," matters that are utterly unfamiliar to bin Laden and his associates, or other radical Islamists like those convicted for the 1993 bombings, and of no concern to them, just as they are, evidently, not concerned by the fact that their atrocities over the years have caused great harm to poor and oppressed people in the Muslim world and elsewhere, again on September II.

Among the immediate victims are Palestinians under military occupation, as the perpetrators surely must have known. Their concerns are different, and bin Laden, at least, has been eloquent enough in expressing them in many interviews: to overthrow the corrupt and repressive regimes of the Arab world and replace them with properly "Islamic" regimes, to support Muslims in their struggles against "infidels" in Saudi Arabia (which he regards as under U.S. occupation), Chechnya, Bosnia, western China, North Africa, and Southeast Asia; maybe elsewhere.

It is convenient for Western intellectuals to speak of "deeper causes" such as hatred of Western values and progress. That is a useful way to avoid questions about the origin of the bin Laden network itself, and about the practices that lead to anger, fear, and desperation throughout the region, and provide a reservoir from which radical Islamic terrorist cells can sometimes draw. Since the answers to these questions are rather clear, and are inconsistent with preferred doctrine, it is better to dismiss the questions as "superficial" and "insignificant," and to turn to "deeper causes" that are in fact more superficial, even insofar as they are relevant.

Should we call what is happening now a war?

There is no precise definition of "war." People speak of the "war on poverty," the "drug war," etc. What is taking shape is not a conflict among states, though it could become one.

Can we talk of the clash between two civilizations?

This is fashionable talk, but it makes little sense. Suppose
we briefly review some familiar history. The most populous
Islamic state is Indonesia, a favorite of the United States
ever since Suharto took power in 1965, as army-led massacres slaughtered hundreds of thousands of people, mostly
landless peasants, with the assistance of the U.S. and with
an outburst of euphoria from the West that is so embarrassing in retrospect that it has been effectively wiped out
of memory. Suharto remained "our kind of guy," as the
Clinton administration called him, as he compiled one of
the most horrendous records of slaughter, torture, and other
abuses of the late 20th century. The most extreme Islamic
fundamentalist state, apart from the Taliban, is Saudi Arabia, a U.S. client since its founding. In the 1980s, the U.S.
along with Pakistani intelligence (helped by Saudi Arabia,
Britain, and others), recruited, armed, and trained the most
extreme Islamic fundamentalists they could find to cause
maximal harm to the Soviets in Afghanistan. As Simon
Jenkins observes in the London *Times*, those efforts
"destroyed a moderate regime and created a fanatical one,
from groups recklessly financed by the Americans" (most
of the funding was probably Saudi). One of the indirect
beneficiaries was Osama bin Laden.

Also in the 1980s, the U.S. and U.K. gave strong support to their friend and ally Saddam Hussein—more
secular, to be sure, but on the Islamic side of the "clash"—
right through the period of his worst atrocities, including
the gassing of the Kurds, and beyond.

Also in the 1980s the U.S. fought a major war in Central America, leaving some 200,000 tortured and mutilated corpses, millions of orphans and refugees, and four countries devastated. A prime target of the U.S. attack was the Catholic Church, which had committed the grievous sin of adopting "the preferential option for the poor."

In the early 90s, primarily for cynical power reasons, the U.S. selected Bosnian Muslims as their Balkan clients, hardly to their benefit.

Without continuing, exactly where do we find the divide between "civilizations." Are we to conclude that there is a "clash of civilizations" with the Latin American Catholic Church on one side, and the U.S. and the Muslim world, including its most murderous and fanatic religious elements, on the other side? I do not of course suggest any such absurdity. But exactly what are we to conclude, on rational grounds?

Do you think we are using the word "civilization" properly? Would a really civilized world lead us to a global war like this?

No civilized society would tolerate anything I have just mentioned, which is of course only a tiny sample even of U.S. history, and European history is even worse. And surely no "civilized world" would plunge the world into a major war instead of following the means prescribed by international law, following ample precedents.

The attacks have been called an act of hate. Where do you think this hate comes from?

For the radical Islamists mobilized by the CIA and its associates, the hate is just what they express. The U.S. was happy to support their hatred and violence when it was directed against U.S. enemies; it is not happy when the hatred it helped nurture is directed against the U.S. and its allies, as it has been, repeatedly, for 20 years. For the population of the region, quite a distinct category, the reasons for their feelings are not obscure. The sources of those sentiments are also quite well known.

What do you suggest the citizens of the Western world could do to bring back peace?

That depends what these citizens want. If they want an escalating cycle of violence, in the familiar pattern, they should certainly call on the U.S. to fall into bin Laden's "diabolical trap" and massacre innocent civilians. If they want to reduce the level of violence, they should use their influence to direct the great powers in a very different course, the one I outlined earlier, which, again, has ample precedents. That includes a willingness to examine what lies behind the atrocities. One often hears that we must not consider these matters, because that would be justification for terrorism, a position so foolish and destructive as scarcely to merit comment, but unfortunately common. But if we do not wish to contribute to escalating the cycle of violence, with targets among the rich and powerful as well, that is exactly what we must do, as in all other cases, including those familiar enough in Spain. [*Editor's note: Chomsky is being interviewed by the Spanish press, and thus his references to Spain.*]

Did the U.S. "ask for" these attacks? Are they consequences of American politics?

The attacks are not "consequences" of U.S. policies in any direct sense. But indirectly, of course they are consequences; that is not even controversial. There seems little doubt that the perpetrators come from the terrorist network that has its roots in the mercenary armies that were organized, trained, and armed by the CIA, Egypt, Pakistan, French intelligence, Saudi Arabian funding, and others. The backgrounds of all of this remain somewhat murky. The organization of these forces started in 1979, if we can believe President Carter's National Security Adviser Zbigniew Brzezinski. He claimed, maybe he was just bragging, that in mid-1979 he had instigated secret support for Mujahidin fighting against the government of Afghanistan in an effort to draw the Russians into what he called an "Afghan trap," a phrase worth remembering. He's very proud of the fact that they did fall into the "Afghan trap" by sending military forces to support the government six months later, with consequences that we know. The United States, along with its allies, assembled a huge mercenary army, maybe 100,000 or more, and they drew from the most militant sectors they could find, which happened to be radical Islamists, what are called here Islamic fundamentalists, from all over, most of them not from Afghanistan. They're called "Afghanis," but like bin Laden, many come from elsewhere.

Bin Laden joined sometime in the 1980s. He was involved in the funding networks, which probably are the ones which still exist. They fought a holy war against the Russian occupiers. They carried terror into Russian territory. They won the war and the Russian invaders withdrew. The war was not their only activity. In 1981, forces based in those same groups assassinated President Sadat of Egypt, who had been instrumental in setting them up. In 1983, one suicide bomber, maybe with connections to the same forces, essentially drove the U.S. military out of Lebanon. And it continued.

By 1989, they had succeeded in their Holy War in Afghanistan. As soon as the U.S. established a permanent military presence in Saudi Arabia, bin Laden and the rest announced that from their point of view, that was comparable to the Russian occupation of Afghanistan and they turned their guns on the Americans, as had already happened in 1983 when the U.S. had military forces in Lebanon. Saudi Arabia is a major enemy of the bin Laden network, just as Egypt is. That's what they want to overthrow, what they call the un-Islamic governments of Egypt, Saudi Arabia, other states of the Middle East, and North Africa. And it continued.

In 1997 they murdered roughly sixty tourists in Egypt and destroyed the Egyptian tourist industry. And they've been carrying out activities all over the region, North Africa, East Africa, the Middle East, the Balkans, Central Asia, western China, Southeast Asia, the U.S., for years. That's one group. And that is an outgrowth of the wars of the 1980s and, if you can believe Brzezinski, even before, when they set the "Afghan trap." Furthermore, as is common knowledge among anyone who pays attention to the region, the terrorists draw from a reservoir of desperation, anger, and frustration that extends from rich to poor, from secular to radical Islamist. That it is rooted in no small measure in U.S. policies is evident and constantly articulated to those willing to listen.

You said that the main practitioners of terrorism are countries like the U.S. that use violence for political motives. When and where?

I find the question baffling. As I've said elsewhere, the U.S. is, after all, the only country condemned by the World Court for international terrorism—for "the unlawful use of force" for political ends, as the Court put it—ordering the U.S. to terminate these crimes and pay substantial reparations. The U.S. of course dismissed the Court's judgment with contempt, reacting by escalating the terrorist war against Nicaragua and vetoing a Security Council resolution calling on all states to observe international law (and voting alone, with Israel and in one case El Salvador, against similar General Assembly resolutions). The terrorist war expanded in accordance with the official policy of attacking "soft targets"—undefended civilian targets, like agricultural collectives and health clinics—instead of engaging the Nicaraguan army. The terrorists were able to carry out these instructions, thanks to the complete control of Nicaraguan air space by the U.S. and the advanced communications equipment provided to them by their supervisors.

It should also be recognized that these terrorist actions were widely approved. One prominent commentator, Michael Kinsley, at the liberal extreme of the mainstream, argued that we should not simply dismiss State Department justifications for terrorist attacks on "soft targets": a "sensible policy" must "meet the test of cost-benefit analysis," he wrote, an analysis of "the amount of blood and misery that will be poured in, and the likelihood that democracy will emerge at the other end"—"democracy" as the U.S. understands the term, an interpretation illustrated quite clearly in the region. It is taken for granted that U.S. elites have the right to conduct the analysis and pursue the project if it passes their tests.

Even more dramatically, the idea that Nicaragua should have the right to defend itself was considered outrageous across the mainstream political spectrum in the United States. The U.S. pressured allies to stop providing Nicaragua with arms, hoping that it would turn to Russia, as it did; that provides the right propaganda images. The Reagan administration repeatedly floated rumors that Nicaragua was receiving jet fighters from Russia—to protect its airspace, as everyone knew, and to prevent U.S. terrorist attacks against "soft targets." The rumors were false, but the reaction was instructive. The doves questioned the rumors, but said that if they are true, of course we must bomb Nicaragua, because it will be a threat to our security. Database searches revealed that there was scarcely a hint that Nicaragua had the right to defend itself. That tells us quite a lot about the deep-seated "culture of terrorism" that prevails in Western civilization.

This is by no means the most extreme example; I mention it because it is uncontroversial, given the World Court decision, and because the failed efforts of Nicaragua to pursue lawful means, instead of setting off bombs in Washington, provide a model for today, not the only one. Nicaragua was only one component of Washington's terrorist wars in Central America in that terrible decade, leaving hundreds of thousands dead and four countries in ruins.

During the same years the U.S. was carrying out large-scale terrorism elsewhere, including the Middle East: to cite one example, the car bombing in Beirut in 1985 outside a mosque, timed to kill the maximum number of civilians, with 80 dead and 250 casualties, aimed at a Muslim sheikh, who escaped. And it supported much worse terror: for example, Israel's invasion of Lebanon that killed some 18,000 Lebanese and Palestinian civilians, not in self-defense, as was conceded at once; and the vicious "iron fist" atrocities of the years that followed, directed against "terrorist villagers," as Israel put it. And the subsequent invasions of 1993 and 1996, both strongly supported by the U.S. (until the international reaction to the Qana massacre in 1996, which caused Clinton to draw back). The post-1982 toll in Lebanon alone is probably another 20,000 civilians.

In the 1990s, the U.S. provided 80 percent of the arms for Turkey's counterinsurgency campaign against Kurds in its southeast region, killing tens of thousands, driving 2-3 million out of their homes, leaving 3,500 villages destroyed (7 times Kosovo under NATO bombs), and with every imaginable atrocity. The arms flow had increased sharply in 1984 as Turkey launched its terrorist attack and began to decline to previous levels only in 1999, when the atrocities had achieved their goal. In 1999, Turkey fell from its position as the leading recipient of U.S. arms (Israel-Egypt aside), replaced by

Colombia, the worst human rights violator in the hemisphere in the 1990s and by far the leading recipient of U.S. arms and training, following a consistent pattern.

In East Timor, the U.S. (and Britain) continued their support of the Indonesian aggressors, who had already wiped out about 1/3 of the population with their crucial help. That continued right through the atrocities of 1999, with thousands murdered even before the early September assault that drove 85 percent of the population from their homes and destroyed 70 percent of the country—while the Clinton administration kept to its position that "it is the responsibility of the government of Indonesia, and we don't want to take that responsibility away from them."

That was September 8, well after the worst of the September atrocities had been reported. By then Clinton was coming under enormous pressure to do something to mitigate the atrocities, mainly from Australia but also from home. A few days later, the Clinton administration indicated to the Indonesian generals that the game was over. They instantly reversed course. They had been strongly insisting that they would never withdraw from East Timor, and they were in fact setting up defenses in Indonesian West Timor (using British jets, which Britain continued to send) to repel a possible intervention force. When Clinton gave the word, they reversed course 180 degrees and announced that they would withdraw, allowing an Australian-led UN peacekeeping force to enter unopposed by the army. The course of events reveals very graphically the latent power that was always available to Washington, and that could have been used to prevent twenty-five years of virtual genocide culminating in the new wave of atrocities from early 1999. Instead, successive U.S. administrations, joined by Britain and others in 1978 when atrocities were peaking, preferred to lend crucial support, military and diplomatic, to the killers—to "our kind of guy," as the Clinton administration described the murderous President Suharto. These facts, clear and dramatic, identify starkly the prime locus of responsibility for these terrible crimes of twenty-five years—in fact, continuing in miserable refugee camps in Indonesian West Timor.

We also learn a lot about Western civilization from the fact that this shameful record is hailed as evidence of our new dedication to "humanitarian intervention," and a justification for the NATO bombing of Serbia.

I have already mentioned the devastation of Iraqi civilian society, with about 1 million deaths, over half of them young children, according to reports that cannot simply be ignored.

This is only a small sample.

I am, frankly, surprised that the question can even be raised—particularly in France, which has made its own contributions to massive state terror and violence, surely not unfamiliar. [*Editor's note: Chomsky is being interviewed by French media here, thus the references to France.*]

Are reactions unanimous in the U.S.? Do you share them, partly or completely?

If you mean the reaction of outrage over the horrifying criminal assault, and sympathy for the victims, then the reactions are virtually unanimous everywhere, including the Muslim countries. Of course every sane person shares them completely, not "partly." If you are referring to the calls for a murderous assault that will surely kill many innocent people—and, incidentally, answer bin Laden's most fervent prayers—than there is no such "unanimous reaction," despite superficial impressions that one might derive from watching TV. As for me, I join a great many others in opposing such actions. A great many.

What majority sentiment is, no one can really say: it is too diffuse and complex. But "unanimous"? Surely not, except with regard to the nature of the crime.

Do you condemn terrorism? How can we decide which act is terrorism and which one is an act of resistance against a tyrant or an occupying force? In which category do you "classify" the recent strike against the U.S.A.?

I understand the term "terrorism" exactly in the sense defined in official U.S. documents: "the calculated use of violence or threat of violence to attain goals that are political, religious, or ideological in nature. This is done through intimidation, coercion, or instilling fear." In accord with this—entirely appropriate—definition, the recent attack on the U.S. is certainly an act of terrorism; in fact, a horrifying terrorist crime. There is scarcely any disagreement about this throughout the world, nor should there be.

But alongside the literal meaning of the term, as just quoted from U.S. official documents, there is also a propagandistic usage, which unfortunately is the standard one: the term "terrorism" is used to refer to terrorist acts committed by enemies against us or our allies. This propagandistic use is virtually universal. Everyone "condemns terrorism" in this sense of the term. Even the Nazis harshly condemned terrorism and carried out what they called "counter-terrorism" against the terrorist partisans.

The United States basically agreed. It organized and conducted similar "counter-terrorism" in Greece and elsewhere in the postwar years. [*Editor's note: The interviewer here is a Greek journalist, thus Chomsky's references to Greece.*] Furthermore, U.S. counterinsurgency programs drew quite explicitly from the Nazi model, which was treated with respect: Wehrmacht officers were consulted and their manuals were used in designing postwar counterinsurgency programs worldwide, typically called "counter-terrorism," matters studied in important work by Michael McClintock, in particular. Given these conventions, even the very same people and actions can quickly shift from "terrorists" to "freedom fighters" and back again. That's been happening right next door to Greece in recent years.

The KLA-UCK were officially condemned by the U.S. as "terrorists" in 1998, because of their attacks on Serb police and civilians in an effort to elicit a disproportionate and brutal Serbian response, as they openly declared. As late as January 1999, the British—the most hawkish element in NATO on this matter—believed that the KLA-UCK was responsible for more deaths than Serbia, which is hard to believe, but at least tells us something about perceptions at high levels in NATO. If one can trust the voluminous documentation provided by the State Department, NATO, the OSCE, and other Western sources, nothing materially changed on the ground until the withdrawal of the KVM monitors and the bombing in late March 1999. But policies did change: the U.S. and U.K. decided to launch an attack on Serbia, and the "terrorists" instantly became "freedom fighters." After the war, the "freedom fighters" and their close associates became "terrorists," "thugs," and "murderers" as they carried out what from their point of view are similar actions for similar reasons in Macedonia, a U.S. ally.

Everyone condemns terrorism, but we have to ask what they mean. You can find the answer to your question about my views in many books and articles that I have written about terrorism in the past several decades, though I use the term in the literal sense, and hence condemn all terrorist actions, not only those that are called "terrorist" for propagandistic reasons.

Is Islam dangerous to Western civilization? Does the Western way of life pose a threat to mankind?

The question is too broad and vague for me to answer. It should be clear, however, that the U.S. does not regard Islam as an enemy, or conversely.

As for the "Western way of life," it includes a great variety of elements, many highly admirable, many adopted with enthusiasm in the Islamic world, many criminal and even a threat to human survival.

As for "Western civilization," perhaps we can heed the words attributed to Gandhi when asked what he thought about "Western civilization": he said that it might be a good idea.

7.

Considerable Restraint?

Based on interviews with Michael Albert on September 30, 2001, and Greg Ruggiero on October 5, 2001.

Q: There has been an immense movement of troops and extreme use of military rhetoric, up to comments about terminating governments, etc. Yet, now there appears to be considerable restraint . . . what happened?

CHOMSKY: From the first days after the attack, the Bush administration has been warned by NATO leaders, specialists on the region, and presumably its own intelligence agencies (not to speak of many people like you and me) that if they react with a massive assault that kills many innocent people, they will be fulfilling the ardent wishes of bin Laden and others like him. That would be true—perhaps even more so—if they happen to kill bin Laden, still without having provided credible evidence of his involvement in the crimes of September 11. He would then be perceived as a martyr even among the enormous majority of Muslims who deplore those crimes. If he is silenced by imprisonment or death, his voice will continue to resound on tens of thousands of cassettes already circulat-

ing throughout the Muslim world, and in many interviews, including late September. An assault that kills
innocent Afghans would be virtually a call for new recruits
to the horrendous cause of the bin Laden network and
other graduates of the terrorist forces set up by the CIA
and its associates 20 years ago to fight a Holy War against
the Russians, meanwhile following their own agenda.

The message appears to have finally gotten through to
the Bush administration, which has—wisely from their
point of view—chosen to follow a different course.

However, "restraint" seems to me a questionable word. On
September 16, the *New York Times* reported that "Washington
has also demanded [from Pakistan] a cutoff of fuel supplies . . . and the elimination of truck convoys that provide
much of the food and other supplies to Afghanistan's civilian
population." Remarkably, that report elicited no detectable
reaction in the West, a grim reminder of the nature of the
Western civilization that leaders and intellectual elites claim
to uphold. In the following days, those demands were implemented. On September 27, the same correspondent reported
that officials in Pakistan "said today that they would not relent
in their decision to seal off the country's 1,400-mile border
with Afghanistan, a move requested by the Bush administration because, the officials said, they wanted to be sure that
none of Mr. bin Laden's men were hiding among the huge
tide of refugees" (John Burns, Islamabad). "The threat of military strikes forced the removal of international aid workers,
crippling assistance programs"; refugees reaching Pakistan
"after arduous journeys from Afghanistan are describing
scenes of desperation and fear at home as the threat of Amer-

ican-led military attacks turns their long-running misery into a potential catastrophe" (Douglas Frantz, *New York Times*, September 30). "The country was on a lifeline," one evacuated aid worker reports, "and we just cut the line" (John Sifton, *New York Times Magazine*, September 30).

According to the world's leading newspaper, then, Washington acted at once to ensure the death and suffering of enormous numbers of Afghans, millions of them already on the brink of starvation. That is the meaning of the words just quoted, and many others like them.

Huge numbers of miserable people have been fleeing to the borders in terror after Washington's threat to bomb the shreds of existence remaining in Afghanistan and to convert the Northern Alliance into a heavily armed military force. They naturally fear that if these forces are unleashed, now greatly reinforced, they might renew the atrocities that tore the country apart and led much of the population to welcome the Taliban when they drove out the murderous warring factions that Washington and Moscow now hope to exploit for their own purposes.

Their record is atrocious. The executive director of the arms division at Human rights Watch, Joost Hiltermann, a Middle East specialist, describes the period of their rule from 1992 to 1995 as "the worst in Afghanistan's history." Human Rights groups report that their warring factions killed tens of thousands of civilians, also committing mass rapes and other atrocities. That continued as they were driven out by the Taliban. To take one case, in 1997 they murdered 3,000 prisoners of war, according to HRW, and they have also carried out massive ethnic cleansing in areas suspected of

Taliban sympathies, leaving a trail of burned-out villages (see, among others, Charles Sennott, *Boston Globe*, October 6).

There is also every reason to suppose that Taliban terror, already awful enough, sharply increased in response to the same expectations that caused the refugee flight.

When they reach the sealed borders, refugees are trapped to die in silence. Only a trickle can escape through remote mountain passes. How many have already succumbed we cannot guess. Within a few weeks the harsh winter will arrive. There are some reporters and aid workers in the refugee camps across the borders. What they describe is horrifying enough, but they know, and we know, that they are seeing the lucky ones, the few who were able to escape—and who express their hopes that "even the cruel Americans must feel some pity for our ruined country" and relent in this silent genocide (*Boston Globe*, September 27, page 1).

The UN World Food Program was able to truck hundreds of tons of food into Afghanistan in early October, though it estimated that this accounted for only 15 percent of the country's needs after the withdrawal of the international staff and the three-week break in deliveries following 9-11. However, the WFP announced that it halted all food convoys and all distribution of food by its local staff because of the air strikes of October 7. "The nightmare scenario of up to 1.5 million refugees flooding out of the country moved a step closer to reality" after the attacks, AFP reported, citing aid officials. A WFP director said that after the bombing, the threat of humanitarian catastrophe, already severe, had "increased on a scale of magnitude I don't even want to think about." "We are facing a humanitarian crisis of epic proportions in Afghanistan with 7.5 million short of food and at risk of starvation," a spokesman for the UNHCR warned. All agencies regard air drops as a last resort, far preferring truck delivery, which they say would be possible to most of the country. The *Financial Times* reported that senior officials of NGOs were "scathing" and "scornful" in their reaction to the much-heralded U.S. air drop, dismissing it as a "propaganda ploy rather than a way to get aid to Afghans who really need help," a "propaganda tool" that was "exploiting humanitarian aid for cynical propaganda purposes" while the air strikes "had halted the only means of getting large volumes of food to Afghans—overland truck convoys" of the WFP ("UN concern as airstrikes bring relief effort to halt," "Relief workers hit at linking of food drops with air raids," *Financial Times*, October 9, citing Oxfam, Doctors without Borders, Christian Aid, Save the Children Fund, and UN officials). Aid agencies were "scathingly critical about the nightly US airdrops." "They might as well just drop leaflets," a British aid worker commented, referring to the propaganda messages on the packages. "WFP officials say [air drops] would require workers on the ground to collect the food" and distribute it, and "must be made in daylight" and with adequate forewarning ("Scepticism grows over US food airdrops," *Financial Times*, October 10).

If these reactions are accurate, then the immediate effect of the bombing and the air drops of food that accompanied it was therefore to reduce significantly the food supplies available to the starving population, at least in the short term, while bringing the "nightmare scenario" a step closer. One can only hope that the torture will stop before the worst fears are realized, and that the suspension of desperately-needed food will be brief.

It is not easy to be optimistic about that, considering the attitudes expressed. For example, a *New York Times* report on an inside page casually mentions that "by the arithmetic of the United Nations, there will soon be 7.5 million Afghans in acute need of even a loaf of bread, . . . but with bombs falling," food deliveries by truck (the only significant contribution) have reduced by about half and there are only a few weeks before the harsh winter reduces the possibility of food distribution sharply (Barry Bearak, Oct. 15, B8). The further calculations are not given, but are not hard to carry out. Whatever happens, the fact that these appear to be the casual assumptions of planning and commentary defies comment.

We should also bear in mind that from the first days after the 9-11 attack, there has been nothing to stop massive food drops by air to the people imprisoned within the country that is once again being cruelly tortured; nor, apparently, the delivery of far greater quantities by truck, as the UN effort showed before it was suspended.

Whatever policies are adopted from this point on, a humanitarian catastrophe has already taken place, with worse to come. Perhaps the most apt description was given by the wonderful and courageous Indian writer and activist Arundhati Roy, referring to Operation Infinite Justice proclaimed by the Bush administration: "Witness the infinite justice of the new century. Civilians starving to death while they're waiting to be killed" (*Guardian*, September 29).

Her judgment loses no force from the fact that administration PR specialists realized that the phrase "infinite justice," suggesting the self-image of divinity, was another propaganda error, like "crusade." It was therefore changed to "enduring freedom"—in the light of the historical record, a phrase that defies comment.

The UN has indicated that the threat of starvation in Afghanistan is enormous. International criticism on this score has grown and now the U.S. and Britain are talking about providing food aid to ward off hunger. Are they caving in to dissent in fact, or only in appearance? What is their motivation? What will be the scale and impact of their efforts?

The United Nations estimates that some 7-8 million are at risk of imminent starvation. The *New York Times* reports in a small item (September 25) that nearly six million Afghans depend on food aid from the UN, as well as 3.5 million in refugee camps outside, many of whom fled just before the borders were sealed. The item reported that some food is being sent to the camps outside Afghanistan. Planners and commentators surely realize that they must do something to present themselves as humanitarians seeking to avert the awesome tragedy that unfolded at once after the threat of bombing and military attack, and the sealing of the borders they demanded. "Experts also urge the United States to improve its image by increasing aid to Afghan refugees, as well as by helping to rebuild the economy" (*Christian Science Monitor*, September 28). Even without PR specialists to instruct them, administration officials must comprehend that they should send some food to the refugees who made it across the border, and make at least some gesture towards providing food to starving people within: in order "to save lives" but also to "help the effort to find terror groups inside Afghanistan" (*Boston Globe*, September 27, quoting a Pentagon official, who describes this as "winning the hearts and minds of the people"). The *New York Times* editors picked up the same theme the following day, twelve days after the journal reported that the murderous operations were being put into effect.

On the scale of aid, one can only hope that it is enormous, or the human tragedy may be immense in a few weeks. If the government is sensible, there will be at least a show of the "massive air drops" that officials mention but have still not carried out as of September 30, not for lack of means.

International legal institutions would likely ratify efforts to arrest and try bin Laden and others, supposing guilt could be shown, including the use of force. Why does the U.S. avoid this recourse? Is it only a matter of not wishing to legitimate an approach that could be used, as well, against our acts of terrorism, or are other factors at play?

Much of the world has been asking the U.S. to provide some evidence to link bin Laden to the crime, and if such evidence could be provided, it would not be difficult to rally enormous support for an international effort, under the rubric of the UN, to apprehend and try him and his collaborators.

It's not impossible that this could be done through

diplomatic means, as the Taliban have been indicating in various ways, though these moves are dismissed with contempt in favor of the use of force.

However, providing credible evidence is no simple matter. Even if bin Laden and his network are involved in the crimes of 9-11, it may be hard to produce credible evidence. And for all we know, most of the perpetrators may have killed themselves in their awful missions.

How hard it is to provide credible evidence was revealed on October 5, when British Prime Minister Tony Blair proclaimed with great fanfare that there is now "absolutely no doubt" about the responsibility of bin Laden and the Taliban, releasing documentation based on what must be the most intensive investigative effort in history, combining the resources of all Western intelligence agencies and others. Despite the prima facie plausibility of the charge, and the unprecedented effort to establish it, the documentation is surprisingly thin. Only a small fraction of it even bears on the Sept. 11 crimes, and that little would surely not be taken seriously if presented as a charge against Western state criminals or their clients. The *Wall Street Journal* accurately described the documents as "more like a charge than detailed evidence," relegating the report to a back page. The *Journal* also points out, accurately, that it doesn't matter, quoting a senior U.S. official who says that "The criminal case is irrelevant. The plan is to wipe out Mr. bin Laden and his organization." The point of the documentation is to allow Blair, the Secretary General of NATO, and others to assure the world that the evidence is "clear and compelling."

It is highly unlikely that the case presented will be credible to people of the Middle East, as reported at once by Robert Fisk, or to others who look beyond headlines. Governments and their organizations, in contrast, have their own reasons to fall into line. One might ask why Washington's propaganda specialists chose to have Blair present the case: perhaps to sustain the image of holding back some highly convincing evidence for "security reasons," or in the hope that he would strike properly Churchillian poses.

In the background there are other minefields that planners must step through with care. To quote Arundhati Roy again, "The Taliban's response to U.S. demands for the extradition of bin Laden has been uncharacteristically reasonable: produce the evidence, then we'll hand him over. President Bush's response is that the demand is non-negotiable." She also adds one of the many reasons why this framework is unacceptable to Washington: "While talks are on for the extradition of CEOs, can India put in a side request for the extradition of Warren Anderson of the U.S.? He was the chairman of Union Carbide, responsible for the Bhopal gas leak that killed 16,000 people in 1984. We have collated the necessary evidence. It's all in the files. Could we have him, please?"

We needn't invent examples. The Haitian government has been asking the U.S. to extradite Emmanuel Constant, one of the most brutal of the paramilitary leaders while the (first) Bush and Clinton administrations (contrary to many illusions) were lending tacit support to the ruling junta and its rich constituency. Constant was tried in absentia in

Haiti and sentenced to life in prison for his role in massacres. Has he been extradited? Does the matter evoke any detectable mainstream concern? To be sure, there are good reasons for the negative answers: extradition might lead to exposure of links that could be embarrassing in Washington. And after all, he was a leading figure in the slaughter of only about 5,000 people—relative to population, a few hundred thousand in the United States.

Such observations elicit frenzied tantrums at the extremist fringes of Western opinion, some of them called "the left." But for Westerners who have retained their sanity and moral integrity, and for many of the traditional victims, they are meaningful and instructive. Government leaders presumably understand that.

The single example that Roy mentions is only the beginning, of course; and it is one of the lesser examples, not only because of the scale of the atrocity, but because it was not explicitly a crime of state. Suppose Iran were to request the extradition of high officials of the Carter and Reagan administrations, refusing to present the ample evidence of the crimes they were implementing—and it surely exists. Or suppose Nicaragua were to demand the extradition of the newly-appointed ambassador to the UN, a man whose record includes his service as "proconsul" (as he was often called) in the virtual fiefdom of Honduras, where he surely was aware of the atrocities of the state terrorists he was supporting; and more significantly, includes his duties as local overseer of the terrorist war against Nicaragua, launched from Honduran bases. Would the U.S. agree to extradite them? Would the request even elicit ridicule?

That is only the barest beginning. The doors are better left closed, just as it is best to maintain the impressive silence that has reigned since the appointment of a leading figure in managing the operations condemned as terrorism by the highest existing international bodies to lead a "war on terrorism." Even Jonathan Swift would be speechless.

That may be the reason why administration publicity experts preferred the ambiguous term "war" to the more explicit term "crime"—"crime against humanity" as Robert Fisk, Mary Robinson, and others have accurately depicted it.

If the Taliban regime falls and bin Laden or someone they claim is responsible is captured or killed, what next? What happens to Afghanistan? What happens more broadly in other regions?

The sensible administration plan would be to pursue the ongoing program of silent genocide, combined with humanitarian gestures to arouse the applause of the usual chorus who are called upon to sing the praises of the noble leaders who are dedicated to "principles and values" for the first time in history and are leading the world to a "new era" of idealism and commitment to "ending inhumanity" everywhere. Turkey is now very pleased to join Washington's "War against Terror," even to send ground troops. The reason, Prime Minister Ecevit said, is that Turkey owes the U.S. a special "debt of gratitude" because unlike European countries, Washington "had backed Ankara in its struggle against terrorism." He is referring to the 15-year war, peaking in the late 1990s with increasing U.S. aid, which left tens of thousands dead, 2-3 million refugees, and

3,500 towns and villages destroyed (seven times Kosovo under NATO bombs). Turkey was also lavishly praised and rewarded by Washington for joining the humanitarian effort in Kosovo, using the same U.S.-supplied F-16s that it had employed with such effectiveness in its own huge ethnic cleansing and state terror operations. The administration might also try to convert the Northern Alliance into a viable force, and may try to bring in other warlords hostile to it, like Washington's former favorite Gulbuddin Hekmatyar, now in Iran. Presumably British and U.S. commandos will undertake missions within Afghanistan, along with selective bombing, but scaled down so as not to recruit new forces for the cause of the radical Islamists.

U.S. campaigns should not be too casually compared to the failed Russian invasion of the 1980s. The Russians were facing a major army of perhaps 100,000 men or more, organized, trained, and heavily armed by the CIA and its associates. The U.S. is facing a ragtag force in a country that has already been virtually destroyed by 20 years of horror, for which we bear no slight share of responsibility. The Taliban forces, such as they are, might quickly collapse except for a small hardened core.

And one would expect that the surviving population would welcome an invading force if it is not too visibly associated with the murderous gangs that tore the country to shreds before the Taliban takeover. At this point, many people would be likely to welcome Genghis Khan.

What next? Expatriate Afghans and, apparently, some internal elements who are not part of the Taliban inner circle have been calling for a UN effort to establish some kind of transition government, a process that might succeed in reconstructing something viable from the wreckage, if provided with very substantial reconstruction aid, channeled through independent sources like the UN or credible NGOs. That much should be the minimal responsibility of those who have turned this impoverished country into a land of terror, desperation, corpses, and mutilated victims. That could happen, but not without very substantial popular efforts in the rich and powerful societies. For the present, any such course has been ruled out by the Bush administration, which has announced that it will not be engaged in "nation building"—or, it seems so far (September 30), an effort that would be far more honorable and humane: substantial support, without interference, for "nation building" by others who might actually achieve some success in the enterprise. But current refusal to consider this decent course is not graven in stone.

What happens in other regions depends on internal factors, on the policies of foreign actors (the U.S. primary among them, for obvious reasons), and the way matters proceed in Afghanistan. One can say little with much confidence, but for many of the possible courses it is possible to make some reasonable assessments about the likely outcome—and there are a great many possibilities, too many to try to review in brief comments.

In order to shape an international alliance, the U.S. has suddenly shifted positions with a number of countries in the Middle East, Africa, and Asia, offering a variety of political, military and monetary packages in exchange for forms of sup-

*port. How might these sudden moves be affecting the political
dynamics in those regions?*

Washington is stepping very delicately. We have to
remember what is at stake: the world's major energy
reserves, primarily in Saudi Arabia but throughout the
Gulf region, along with not inconsiderable resources in
Central Asia. Though a minor factor, Afghanistan has
been discussed for years as a possible site for pipelines that
will aid the U.S. in the complex maneuvering over control
of Central Asian resources. North of Afghanistan, the
states are fragile and violent. Uzbekistan is the most
important. It has been condemned by Human Rights
Watch for serious atrocities and is fighting its own internal Islamic insurgency. Tajikistan is similar, and is also a
major drug-trafficking outlet to Europe, primarily in con-
nection with the Northern Alliance, which controls much
of the Afghan-Tajikistan border and has apparently been
the major source of drugs since the Taliban virtually eliminated poppy production. Flight of Afghans to the north
could lead to all sorts of internal problems. Pakistan, which
has been the main supporter of the Taliban, has a strong
internal radical Islamic movement. Its reaction is unpre-
dictable, and potentially dangerous, if Pakistan is visibly
used as a base for U.S. operations in Afghanistan; and
there is much well-advised concern over the fact that Pakistan has nuclear weapons. The Pakistani military, while
eager to obtain military aid from the U.S. (already prom-
ised), is wary, because of stormy past relations, and is also
concerned over a potentially hostile Afghanistan allied

with its enemy to the east, India. They are not pleased that the Northern Alliance is led by Tajiks, Uzbeks, and other Afghan minorities hostile to Pakistan and supported by India, Iran, and Russia, now the U.S. as well.

In the Gulf region, even wealthy and secular elements are bitter about U.S. policies and quietly often express support for bin Laden, whom they detest, as "the conscience of Islam" (*New York Times*, October 5, quoting an international lawyer for multinationals trained in the U.S.). Quietly, because these are highly repressive states; one factor in the general bitterness towards the U.S. is its support for these regimes. Internal conflict could easily spread, with consequences that could be enormous, especially if U.S. control over the huge resources of the region is threatened. Similar problems extend to North Africa and Southeast Asia, particularly Indonesia. Even apart from internal conflict, an increased flow of armaments to the countries of the region increases the likelihood of armed conflict and the flow of weapons to terrorist organizations and narcotraffickers. The governments are eager to join the U.S. "war against terrorism" to gain support for their own state terrorism, often on a shocking scale (Russia and Turkey, to mention only the most obvious examples, though Turkey has always benefited from crucial U.S. support).

Pakistan and India, border countries armed with nuclear weapons, have been eye to eye in serious conflict for years. How might the sudden and intense pressure that the U.S. is exerting in the region impact their already volatile relationship?

The main source of conflict is Kashmir, where India claims to be fighting Islamic terrorism, and Pakistan claims that India is refusing self-determination and has carried out large-scale terrorism itself. All the claims, unfortunately, are basically correct. There have been several wars over Kashmir, the latest one in 1999, when both states had nuclear weapons available; fortunately they were kept under control, but that can hardly be guaranteed. The threat of nuclear war is likely to increase if the U.S. persists in its militarization of space programs (euphemistically described as "missile defense"). These already include support for expansion of China's nuclear forces, in order to gain Chinese acquiescence to the programs. India will presumably try to match China's expansion, then Pakistan, then beyond, including Israel. Its nuclear capacities were described by the former head of the U.S. Strategic Command as "dangerous in the extreme," and one of the prime threats in the region.

"Volatile" is right, maybe worse.

Prior to 9-11, the Bush administration was being fiercely critiqued, ally nations included, for its political "unilateralism"—refusal to sign on to the Kyoto protocol for greenhouse emissions, intention to violate the ABM treaty in order to militarize space with a "missile defense" program, walkout of the racism conference in Durban, South Africa, to name only a few recent examples. Might the sudden U.S. alliance-building effort spawn a new "multilateralism" in which unexpected positive developments—like progress for Palestinians—might advance?

It's worth recalling that Bush's "unilateralism" was an exten-
sion of standard practice. In 1993, Clinton informed the UN
that the U.S. will—as before—act "multilaterally when possible but unilaterally when necessary," and proceeded to do
so. The position was reiterated by UN Ambassador
Madeleine Albright and in 1999 by Secretary of Defense
William Cohen, who declared that the U.S. is committed
to "unilateral use of military power" to defend vital interests,
which include "ensuring uninhibited access to key markets,
energy supplies, and strategic resources," and indeed anything that Washington might determine to be within its
own jurisdiction. But it is true that Bush went beyond, caus-
ing considerable anxiety among allies. The current need to
form a coalition may attenuate the rhetoric but is unlikely
to change the policies. Members of the coalition are
expected to be silent and obedient supporters, not partici-
pants. The U.S. explicitly reserves to itself the right to act
as it chooses, and is carefully avoiding any meaningful
recourse to international institutions, as required by law.
There are gestures to the contrary, but they lack any credibility, though governments will presumably accept them,
bending to power, as they regularly do for their own reasons.
The Palestinians are unlikely to gain anything. On the contrary, the terrorist attack of September 11 was a crushing
blow to them, as they and Israel recognized immediately.

*Since 9-11, Secretary of State Colin Powell has been signalling
that the U.S. may adopt a new stance toward the plight of
Palestinians. What is your reading?*

My reading is exactly that of the officials and other sources quoted towards the end of the front-page story of the *New York Times*. They stressed that Bush-Powell do not even go as far as Clinton's Camp David proposals, lauded in the mainstream here but completely unaccept-able, for reasons discussed accurately in Israel and elsewhere, and as anyone could see by looking at a map—one reason, I suppose, why maps were so hard to find here, though not elsewhere, including Israel. One can find more detail about this in articles at the time of Camp David, including my own, and essays in the collection edited by Roane Carey, *The New Intifada*.

The free flow of information is one of the first casualties of any war. Is the present situation in any way an exception? Exam-ples?

Impediments to free flow of information in countries like the U.S. are rarely traceable to government; rather, to self-censorship of the familiar kind. The current situation is not exceptional—considerably better than the norm, in my opinion.

There are, however, some startling examples of U.S. government efforts to restrict free flow of information abroad. The Arab world has had one free and open news source, the satellite TV news channel Al-Jazeera in Qatar, modeled on BBC, with an enormous audience throughout the Arab-speaking world. It is the sole uncensored source, carrying a great deal of important news and also live debates and a wide range of opinion—broad enough to

include Colin Powell a few days before 9-11 and Israeli
Prime Minister Barak (me too, just to declare an interest).
Al-Jazeera is also "the only international news organization to maintain reporters in the Taliban-controlled part
of Afghanistan" (*Wall Street Journal*). Among other examples, it was responsible for the exclusive filming of the
destruction of Buddhist statues that rightly infuriated the
world. It has also provided lengthy interviews with bin
Laden that I'm sure are perused closely by Western intelligence agencies and are invaluable to others who want to
understand what he is thinking. These are translated and
rebroadcast by BBC, several of them since 9-11.

Al-Jazeera is, naturally, despised and feared by the dicta-
torships of the region, particularly because of its frank
exposures of their human rights records. The U.S. has joined
their ranks. BBC reports that "The U.S. is not the first to
feel aggrieved by Al-Jazeera coverage, which has in the past
provoked anger from Algeria, Morocco, Saudi Arabia,
Kuwait and Egypt for giving airtime to political dissidents."

The emir of Qatar confirmed that "Washington has
asked Qatar to rein in the influential and editorially independent Arabic Al-Jazeera television station," BBC
reported. The emir, who also chairs the Organization of
Islamic Conference that includes 56 countries, informed the
press in Washington that Secretary of State Powell had
pressured him to rein in Al-Jazeera: to "persuade Al-Jazeera
to tone down its coverage," Al-Jazeera reports. Asked about
the reports of censorship, the emir said: "This is true. We
heard from the U.S. administration, and also from the previous U.S. administration" (BBC, October 4 citing Reuters).

The only serious report I noticed of this highly important news is in the *Wall Street Journal* (October 5), which also describes the reaction of intellectuals and scholars throughout the Arab world ("truly appalling," etc.). The report adds, as the Journal has done before, that "many Arab analysts argued that it is, after all, Washington's perceived disregard for human rights in officially pro-American countries such as Saudi Arabia that fuels the rampant anti-Americanism." There has also been remarkably little use of the bin Laden interviews and other material from Afghanistan available from Al-Jazeera.

After Al-Jazeera broadcast a tape of bin Laden that was highly useful to Western propaganda, and instantly received front-page coverage, the channel quickly became famous. The *New York Times* ran a story headlined "An Arab Station Offers Ground-Breaking Coverage" (Elaine Sciolino, October 9). The report lauded the channel as "the Arab world's CNN, with round-the-clock, all news and public affairs programs that reach millions of viewers." "The network has built a reputation for independent groundbreaking reporting that contrasts sharply with other Arab-language television stations," and "has focused on subjects considered subversive in most parts of the Arab world: the absence of democratic institutions, the persecution of political dissidents and the inequality of women." The story notes that "American policy makers have been troubled by Al Jazeera's" broadcasts of bin Laden interviews and the "anti-American oratory" of analysts, guests, and "callers on freewheeling phone-in shows." The rest is unmentioned, though there was a mild editorial admonition the next day.

So yes, there are barriers to free flow of information, but they cannot be blamed on government censorship or pressure, a very marginal factor in the United States.

What do you believe should be the role and priority of social activists concerned about justice at this time? Should we curb our criticisms, as some have claimed, or is this, instead, a time for renewed and enlarged efforts, not only because it is a crisis regarding which we can attempt to have a very important positive impact, but also because large sectors of the public are actually far more receptive than usual to discussion and exploration, even if other sectors are intransigently hostile?

It depends on what these social activists are trying to achieve. If their goal is to escalate the cycle of violence and to increase the likelihood of further atrocities like that of September 11—and, regrettably, even worse ones with which much of the world is all too familiar—then they should certainly curb their analysis and criticisms, refuse to think, and cut back their involvement in the very serious issues in which they have been engaged. The same advice is warranted if they want to help the most reactionary and regressive elements of the political-economic power system to implement plans that will be of great harm to the general population here and in much of the world, and may even threaten human survival. If, on the contrary, the goal of social activists is to reduce the likelihood of further atrocities, and to advance hopes for freedom, human rights, and democracy, then they should follow the opposite course. They should intensify their efforts to inquire into the background factors that lie behind these and other crimes and devote themselves with even more energy to the just causes to which they have already been committed. They should listen when the bishop of the southern Mexican city of San Cristobal de las Casas, who has seen his share of misery and oppression, urges North Americans to "reflect on why they are so hated" after the U.S. "has generated so much violence to protect its economic interests" (Marion Lloyd, Mexico City, *Boston Globe*, September 30).

It is surely more comforting to listen to the words of liberal commentators who assure us that "They hate us because we champion a 'new world order' of capitalism, individualism, secularism and democracy that should be the norm everywhere" (Ronald Steel, *New York Times*, September 14). Or Anthony Lewis, who assures us that the only relevance of our past policies is that they "negatively affect public attitudes in the Arab world toward the coalition's antiterrorism effort" (*New York Times*, October 6). What we have done, he declares confidently, can have had no effect on the goals of the terrorists. What they say is so utterly irrelevant that it can be ignored, and we can also dismiss the conformity between what they have been saying and their specific actions for 20 years of terror—hardly obscure, and reported extensively by serious journalists and scholars. It is a necessary truth, requiring no evidence or argument, that the terrorists seek "the violent transformation of an irremediably sinful and unjust world" and stand only for "apocalyptic nihilism" (quoting Michael Ignatieff with approval). Neither their professed goals and actions nor the clearly articulated attitudes of the population of the region—even highly pro-American Kuwaitis—make the slightest bit of difference. We must therefore disregard anything we have done that might provoke such responses.

More comforting, no doubt, but not more wise, if we care about what lies ahead.

The opportunities are surely there. The shock of the horrendous crimes has already opened elite sectors to reflection of a kind that would have been hard to imagine not long ago, and among the general public that is even more true. Just to speak about personal experience, aside from near-constant interviews with national radio-TV-press in Europe and elsewhere, I have had considerably more access even to mainstream media in the U.S. than ever before, and others report the same experience.

Of course, there will be those who demand silent obedience. We expect that from the ultra-right, and anyone with a little familiarity with history will expect it from some left intellectuals as well, perhaps in an even more virulent form. But it is important not to be intimidated by hysterical ranting and lies and to keep as closely as one can to the course of truth and honesty and concern for the human consequences of what one does, or fails to do. All truisms, but worth bearing in mind.

Beyond the truisms, we turn to specific questions, for inquiry and for action.

Reflections on 9-11

First published by *Aftonbladet* in Sweden, August 2002, and in *11 September—
ett år efteråt* (*September 11—One Year After*) (Stockholm: Aftonbladet, 2002).

It is widely argued that the September 11 terrorist
attacks have changed the world dramatically, that
nothing will be the same as the world enters into an
"age of terror"—the title of a collection of academic essays
by Yale University scholars and others, which regards the
anthrax attack as even more ominous.

There is no doubt that the 9-11 atrocities were an event
of historic importance, not—regrettably—because of their
scale, but because of the choice of innocent victims. It had
been recognized for some time that with new technology,
the industrial powers would probably lose their virtual
monopoly of violence, retaining only an enormous pre-
ponderance. No one could have anticipated the specific
way in which the expectations were fulfilled, but they
were. For the first time in modern history, Europe and its
offshoots were subjected, on home soil, to the kind of
atrocity that they routinely have carried out elsewhere.
The history should be too familiar to review, and though
the West may choose to disregard it, the victims do not.
The sharp break in the traditional pattern surely qualifies

9-11 as a historic event, and the repercussions are sure to be significant.

Several crucial questions arose at once:

(1) who is responsible?

(2) what are the reasons?

(3) what is the proper reaction?

(4) what are the longer-term consequences?

As for (1), it was assumed, plausibly, that the guilty parties were bin Laden and his al-Qaeda network. No one knows more about them than the CIA, which, together with its counterparts among U.S. allies, recruited radical Islamists from many countries and organized them into a military and terrorist force, not to help Afghans resist Russian aggression, which would have been a legitimate objective, but for normal reasons of state, with grim consequences for Afghans after the Mujahidin took control. U.S. intelligence has surely been following the other exploits of these networks closely ever since they assassinated President Sadat of Egypt twenty years ago, and more intensively since the attempt to blow up the World Trade Center and many other targets in a highly ambitious terrorist operation in 1993. Nevertheless, despite what must be the most intensive international intelligence investigation in history, evidence about the perpetrators of 9-11 has been hard to find. Eight months after the bombing, FBI director Robert Mueller, reporting to the press, could say only that U.S. intelligence now "believes" the plot was hatched in Afghanistan, though planned and implemented elsewhere. And long after the source of the anthrax attack was localized to U.S. government weapons laboratories, it has still not been identified. These are indications of how hard it may be to counter acts of terror targeting the rich and powerful in the future. Nevertheless, despite the thin evidence, the initial conclusion about 9-11 is presumably correct.

Turning to (2), scholarship is virtually unanimous in taking the terrorists at their word, which matches their deeds for the past twenty years: their goal, in their terms, is to drive the infidels from Muslim lands, to overthrow the corrupt governments they impose and sustain, and to institute an extremist version of Islam.

More significant, at least for those who hope to reduce the likelihood of further crimes of a similar nature, are the background conditions from which the terrorist organizations arose, and that provide a mass reservoir of sympathetic understanding for at least parts of their message, even among those who despise and fear them. In George Bush's plaintive words, "why do they hate us?" The question is not new, and answers are not hard to find. Forty-five years ago President Eisenhower and his staff discussed what he called the "campaign of hatred against us" in the Arab world, "not by the governments but by the people." The basic reason, the National Security Council advised, is the recognition that the U.S. supports corrupt and brutal governments that block democracy and development, and does so because of its concern "to protect its interest in Near East oil." *The Wall Street Journal* found much the same when it investigated attitudes of wealthy westernized Muslims after 9-11, feelings now exacerbated by specific U.S. policies with regard to Israel/Palestine and Iraq.

Commentators generally prefer a more comforting answer: their anger is rooted in resentment of our freedom and love of democracy, their cultural failings tracing back many centuries, their inability to take part in the form of "globalization" (in which they happily participate), and other such deficiencies. More comforting, perhaps, but not wise.

What about proper reaction, question (3)? The answers are doubtless contentious, but at least the reaction should meet the most elementary moral standards: specifically, if an action is right for us, it is right for others; and if wrong for others, it is wrong for us. Those who reject that standard simply declare that acts are justified by power; they can therefore be ignored in any discussion of appropriateness of action, of right or wrong. One might ask what remains of the flood of commentary on question (3) (debates about "just war," etc.) if this simple criterion is adopted.

To illustrate with a few uncontroversial cases, forty years have passed since President Kennedy ordered that "the terrors of the earth" must be visited upon Cuba until their leadership is eliminated, having violated good form by successful resistance to U.S.-run invasion. The terrors were extremely serious, continuing into the 1990s. Twenty years have passed since President Reagan launched a terrorist war against Nicaragua, conducted with barbaric atrocities and vast destruction, leaving tens of thousands dead and the country ruined perhaps beyond recovery—and also leading to condemnation of the U.S. for international terrorism by the World Court and the UN Security Council (in a resolution the U.S. vetoed). But no one believes that Cuba or Nicaragua had the right to set off bombs in

Washington or New York, or to assassinate U.S. political leaders. And it is all too easy to add many far more severe cases, up to the present.

Accordingly, those who accept elementary moral standards have some work to do to show that the U.S. and Britain were justified in bombing Afghans in order to compel them to turn over people who the U.S. suspected of criminal atrocities, the official war aim, announced by the President as the bombing began; or to overthrow their rulers, the war aim announced several weeks later.

The same moral standard holds of more nuanced proposals about an appropriate response to terrorist atrocities. The respected Anglo-American military historian Michael Howard proposed "a police operation conducted under the auspices of the United Nations . . . against a criminal conspiracy whose members should be hunted down and brought before an international court, where they would receive a fair trial and, if found guilty, be awarded an appropriate sentence" (*Guardian, Foreign Affairs*). That seems reasonable, though we may ask what the reaction would be to the suggestion that the proposal should be applied universally. That is unthinkable, and if the suggestion were to be made, it would arouse outrage and horror.

Similar questions arise with regard to the "Bush doctrine" of "preemptive strike" against suspected threats. It should be noted that the doctrine is not new. High-level planners are mostly holdovers from the Reagan administration, which argued that the bombing of Libya was justified under the UN Charter as "self-defense against future attack." Clinton planners advised "preemptive response" (including nuclear first strike). And the doctrine has earlier precedents. Nevertheless, the bold assertion of such a right is novel, and there is no secret as to whom the threat is addressed. The government and commentators are stressing loud and clear that they intend to apply the doctrine to Iraq. The elementary standard of universality, therefore, would appear to justify Iraqi preemptive terror against the United States. Of course, no one accepts this conclusion. Again, if we are willing to adopt elementary moral principles, obvious questions arise, and must be faced by those who advocate or tolerate the selective version of the doctrine of "preemptive response" that grants the right to those powerful enough to exercise it with little concern for what the world may think. And the burden of proof is not light, as is always true when the threat or use of violence is advocated or tolerated.

There is, of course, an easy counter to such simple arguments: WE are good, and THEY are evil. That useful principle trumps virtually any argument. Analysis of commentary and much of scholarship reveals that its roots commonly lie in that crucial principle, which is not argued but asserted. Occasionally, but rarely, some irritating creatures attempt to confront the core principle with the record of recent and contemporary history. We learn more about prevailing cultural norms by observing the reaction, and the interesting array of barriers erected to deter any lapse into this heresy. None of this, of course, is an invention of contemporary power centers and the dominant intellectual culture. Nonetheless, it merits attention, at least among those who have some interest in understanding where we stand and what may lie ahead.

Let us turn briefly to these last considerations: question (4).

In the longer term, I suspect that the crimes of 9-11 will accelerate tendencies that were already underway: the Bush doctrine, just mentioned, is an illustration. As was predicted at once, governments throughout the world seized upon 9-11 as a window of opportunity to institute or escalate harsh and repressive programs. Russia eagerly joined the "coalition against terror" expecting to receive authorization for its terrible atrocities in Chechnya, and was not disappointed. China happily joined for similar reasons. Turkey was the first country to offer troops for the new phase of the U.S. "war on terror," in gratitude, as the Prime Minister explained, for the U.S. contribution to Turkey's campaign against its miserably-repressed Kurdish population, waged with extreme savagery and relying crucially on a huge flow of U.S. arms. Turkey is highly praised for its achievements in these campaigns of state terror, including some of the worst atrocities of the grisly 1990s, and was rewarded by grant of authority to protect Kabul from terror, funded by the same superpower that provided the military means, and the diplomatic and ideological support, for its recent atrocities. Israel recognized that it would be able to crush Palestinians even more brutally, with even firmer U.S. support. And so on throughout much of the world.

More democratic societies, including the United States, instituted measures to impose discipline on the domestic population and to institute unpopular measures under the guise of "combating terror," exploiting the atmosphere of fear and the demand for "patriotism"—which in practice means: "You shut up and I'll pursue my own agenda relentlessly." The Bush administration used the opportunity to advance its assault against most of the population, and future generations, in service to the narrow corporate interests that dominate the administration to an extent even beyond the norm.

In brief, initial predictions were amply confirmed.

One major outcome is that the United States, for the first time, has major military bases in Central Asia. These are important to position U.S. multinationals favorably in the current "great game" to control the considerable resources of the region, but also to complete the encirclement of the world's major energy resources, in the Gulf region. The U.S. base system targeting the Gulf extends from the Pacific to the Azores, but the closest reliable base before the Afghan war was Diego Garcia. Now that situation is much improved, and forceful intervention, if deemed appropriate, will be greatly facilitated.

The Bush administration perceives the new phase of the "war on terror" (which in many ways replicates the "war on terror" declared by the Reagan administration twenty years earlier) as an opportunity to expand its already overwhelming military advantages over the rest of the world, and to move on to other methods to ensure global dominance. Government thinking was articulated clearly by high officials when Prince Abdullah of Saudi Arabia visited the U.S. in April to urge the administration to pay more attention to the reaction in the Arab world to its strong support for Israeli terror and repression. He was told, in effect, that the U.S. did not care what he or other Arabs think. As the *New York Times* reported, a high official explained that "if he thought we were strong in Desert Storm, we're 10 times as strong today. This was to give him some idea what Afghanistan demonstrated about our capabilities." A senior defense analyst gave a simple gloss: others will "respect us for our toughness and won't mess with us." That stand too has many historical precedents, but in the post-September 11 world it gains new force.

We do not have internal documents, but it is reasonable to speculate that such consequences were one primary goal of the bombing of Afghanistan: to warn the world of what the U.S. can do if someone steps out of line. The bombing of Serbia was undertaken for similar reasons. Its primary goal was to "ensure NATO's credibility," as Blair and Clinton explained—not referring to the credibility of Norway or Italy, but of the U.S. and its prime military client. That is a common theme of statecraft and the literature of international relations; and with some reason, as history amply reveals.

Without continuing, the basic issues of international society seem to me to remain much as they were, but 9-11 surely has induced changes, in some cases, with significant and not very attractive implications.

APPENDIX A

Department of State Report on Foreign Terrorist Organizations

Released by the Office of the Coordinator for Counterterrorism
October 5, 2001

BACKGROUND

The Secretary of State designates Foreign Terrorist Organizations (FTO's), in consultation with the Attorney General and the Secretary of the Treasury. These designations are undertaken pursuant to the Immigration and Nationality Act, as amended by the Antiterrorism and Effective Death Penalty Act of 1996. FTO designations are valid for two years, after which they must be redesignated or they automatically expire. Redesignation after two years is a positive act and represents a determination by the Secretary of State that the organization has continued to engage in terrorist activity and still meets the criteria specified in law.

In October 1997, former Secretary of State Madeleine K. Albright approved the designation of the first 30 groups as Foreign Terrorist Organizations.

In October 1999, Secretary Albright re-certified 27 of these groups' designations but allowed three organizations to drop from the list because their involvement in terrorist activity had ended and they no longer met the criteria for designation.

Secretary Albright designated one new FTO in 1999 (al Qa'ida) and another in 2000 (Islamic Movement of Uzbekistan).

Secretary of State Colin L. Powell has designated two new FTO's (Real IRA and AUC) in 2001.

In October 2001, Secretary Powell re-certified the designation of 26 of the 28 FTO's whose designation was due to expire, and combined two previously designated groups (Kahane Chai and Kach) into one.

Current List of Designated Foreign Terrorist Organizations (as of October 5, 2001):

1. Abu Nidal Organization (ANO)
2. Abu Sayyaf Group
3. Armed Islamic Group (GIA)
4. Aum Shinrikyo
5. Basque Fatherland and Liberty (ETA)
6. Gama'a al-Islamiyya (Islamic Group)
7. HAMAS (Islamic Resistance Movement)
8. Harakat ul-Mujahidin (HUM)
9. Hizballah (Party of God)
10. Islamic Movement of Uzbekistan (IMU)
11. al-Jihad (Egyptian Islamic Jihad)
12. Kahane Chai (Kach)
13. Kurdistan Workers' Party (PKK)
14. Liberation Tigers of Tamil Eelam (LTTE)
15. Mujahedin-e Khalq Organization (MEK)
16. National Liberation Army (ELN)
17. Palestinian Islamic Jihad (PIJ)
18. Palestine Liberation Front (PLF)
19. Popular Front for the Liberation of Palestine (PFLP)

20. PFLP-General Command (PFLP-GC)
21. al-Qaʾida
22. Real IRA
23. Revolutionary Armed Forces of Colombia (FARC)
24. Revolutionary Nuclei (formerly ELA)
25. Revolutionary Organization 17 November
26. Revolutionary People's Liberation Army/Front (DHKP/C)
27. Shining Path (Sendero Luminoso, SL)
28. United Self-Defense Forces of Colombia (AUC)

NOTE: For descriptions of these foreign terrorist organizations,
please refer to "Patterns of Global Terrorism: 2000."

LEGAL CRITERIA FOR DESIGNATION

1. The organization must be foreign.
2. The organization must engage in terrorist activity as defined in Section 212 (a)(3)(B) of the Immigration and Nationality Act.* (see below)
3. The organization's activities must threaten the security of U.S. nationals or the national security (national defense, foreign relations, or the economic interests) of the United States.

EFFECTS OF DESIGNATION

Legal
1. It is unlawful for a person in the United States or subject to the jurisdiction of the United States to provide funds or other material support to a designated FTO.
2. Representatives and certain members of a designated FTO, if they are aliens, can be denied visas or excluded from the United States.
3. U.S. financial institutions must block funds of desig-

nated FTO's and their agents and report the blockage to the Office of Foreign Assets Control, U.S. Department of the Treasury.

Other Effects

1. Deters donations or contributions to named organizations
2. Heightens public awareness and knowledge of terrorist organizations
3. Signals to other governments our concern about named organizations
4. Stigmatizes and isolates designated terrorist organizations internationally

The Process

The Secretary of State makes decisions concerning the designation and redesignation of FTO's following an exhaustive interagency review process in which all evidence of a group's activity, from both classified and open sources, is scrutinized. The State Department, working closely with the Justice and Treasury Departments and the intelligence community, prepares a detailed "administrative record" which documents the terrorist activity of the designated FTO. Seven days before publishing an FTO designation in the Federal Register, the Department of State provides classified notification to Congress.

Under the statute, designations are subject to judicial review. In the event of a challenge to a group's FTO designation in federal court, the U.S. government relies upon the administrative record to defend the Secretary's decision. These administrative records contain intelligence information and are therefore classified.

FTO designations expire in two years unless renewed. The law allows groups to be added at any time following a decision by the Secretary, in consultation with the Attorney General and the Secretary of the Treasury. The Secretary may also revoke designations after determining that there are grounds for doing so and notifying Congress.

* The Immigration and Nationality Act defines terrorist activity to mean: any activity which is unlawful under the laws of the place where it is committed (or which, if committed in the United States, would be unlawful under the laws of the United States or any State) and which involves any of the following:

(I) The highjacking or sabotage of any conveyance (including an aircraft, vessel, or vehicle).

(II) The seizing or detaining, and threatening to kill, injure, or continue to detain, another individual in order to compel a third person (including a governmental organization) to do or abstain from doing any act as an explicit or implicit condition for the release of the individual seized or detained.

(III) A violent attack upon an internationally protected person (as defined in section 1116(b)(4) of title 18, United States Code) or upon the liberty of such a person.

(IV) An assassination.

(V) The use of any—

　(a) biological agent, chemical agent, or nuclear weapon or device, or

　(b) explosive or firearm (other than for mere personal

monetary gain), with intent to endanger, directly or indirectly, the safety of one or more individuals or to cause substantial damage to property.

(VI) A threat, attempt, or conspiracy to do any of the foregoing.

(iii) The term "engage in terrorist activity" means to commit, in an individual capacity or as a member of an organization, an act of terrorist activity or an act which the actor knows, or reasonably should know, affords material support to any individual, organization, or government in conducting a terrorist activity at any time, including any of the following acts:

(I) The preparation or planning of a terrorist activity.

(II) The gathering of information on potential targets for terrorist activity.

(III) The providing of any type of material support, including a safe house, transportation, communications, funds, false documentation or identification, weapons, explosives, or training, to any individual the actor knows or has reason to believe has committed or plans to commit a terrorist activity.

(IV) The soliciting of funds or other things of value for terrorist activity or for any terrorist organization.

(V) The solicitation of any individual for membership in a terrorist organization, terrorist government, or to engage in a terrorist activity.

Department of State
Country Reports on Terrorism 2009

Released by the Office of the Coordinator for Counterterrorism
August 5, 2010

REPLACING PATTERNS OF GLOBAL TERRORISM WITH COUNTRY REPORTS ON TERRORISM

Since September 11, 2001, changes in organization and responsibilities in the intelligence community, combined with the dynamic pace of the global war on terrorism, prompted the Department of State to take a fresh look at *Patterns of Global Terrorism*, its contents and its governing legislation.

For years, statistical data on global terrorism had been published as part of the annual *Patterns* report, the last of which was provided to Congress in April 2004. As the volume of such data began to grow exponentially after 9/11, and the methodologies for analyzing it became more focused, past practices for accumulating statistical information could no longer suffice.

In July 2004, the 9/11 Commission recommended creation of a National Counterterrorism Center (NCTC) to provide an authoritative agency for all-source analysis of global terrorism. The President implemented the recommendation by executive order in August 2004, and the agency was created via the Intelligence Reform and Terrorism Prevention Act the following December.

That law designates the NCTC as the primary organization for analysis and integration of "all intelligence possessed or acquired by the United States government pertaining to terrorism or counterterrorism." It further states that the NCTC would be the government's "shared knowledge bank on known and suspected terrorists and international terror groups, as well as their goals, strategies, capabilities, and networks of contact and support."

Given NCTC's mandate to be the U.S. Government's "shared knowledge bank" for data on global terrorism, and the statutory requirements for the Department of State's annual report to focus primarily on policy issues, it was appropriate to transfer the responsibilities for accumulating statistical information to NCTC. NCTC is already charged with compiling data on terrorist incidents and is the source of any data used to respond to the new statutory requirements.

To reflect the inclusion of NCTC statistical data in the Department of State's annual report and to avoid any confusion resulting from comparing current data with that generated before NCTC's participation, the name of the annual report was changed to *Country Reports on Terrorism* beginning with the 2004 document.

FOREIGN TERRORIST ORGANIZATIONS

Foreign Terrorist Organizations (FTOs) are designated by the Secretary of State in accordance with section 219 of the Immigration and Nationality Act (INA). FTO designations play a critical role in the fight against terrorism and are an effective means of curtailing support for terrorist activities.

IDENTIFICATION

The Department of State continually monitors the activities of terrorist groups around the world in order to identify potential targets for designation. When reviewing potential targets, the Department considers terrorist attacks that a group has carried out, whether the group has engaged in planning and preparations for possible future acts of terrorism, or whether it retains the capability and intent to carry out such acts.

DESIGNATION

Once a target is identified, a detailed "administrative record" is prepared. This record demonstrates that the criteria for designation have been legally satisfied. If the Secretary of State, in consultation with the Attorney General and the Secretary of the Treasury, decides to designate an organization, Congress is notified of the Secretary's intent and given seven days to review the designation, as required by the INA. Upon the expiration of the seven-day waiting period, and in the absence of Congressional action to block the designation, notice of the designation is published in the *Federal Register*, at which point the designation becomes law. An organization designated as an FTO may seek judicial review of the designation in the U. S. Court of Appeals for the District of Columbia Circuit no later than 30 days after the designation is published in the *Federal Register*.

The Intelligence Reform and Terrorism Prevention Act of 2004 provides that a designated FTO may file a petition for revocation two years after its designation date or two years after the determination date of its most recent petition for revocation. In order to provide a basis for revocation, the petitioning FTO must provide evidence that the circumstances forming the basis for the designation have sufficiently changed as to warrant revocation. If no such petition has been filed within a five-year period, the Secretary of State is required to review the designation to determine whether revocation would be appropriate. In addition, the Secretary of State may at any time revoke a designation upon a finding that the circumstances forming the basis for the designation have changed, or that the national security of the United States warrants a revocation. Revocations made by the Secretary of State must undergo the same administrative review and Congressional processes as that of designations. A designation may also be revoked by an Act of Congress.

LEGAL CRITERIA FOR DESIGNATION UNDER SECTION 219 OF THE INA AS AMENDED

1. It must be a *foreign organization*.
2. The organization must *engage in terrorist activity*, as defined in section 212 (a)(3)(B) of the INA (8 U.S.C. § 1182(a)(3)(B)), or *terrorism*, as defined in section 140(d)(2) of the Foreign Relations Authorization Act, Fiscal Years 1988 and 1989 (22 U.S.C. § 2656f(d)(2)), *or retain the capability and intent to engage in terrorist activity or terrorism.*
3. The organization's terrorist activity or terrorism must threaten the security of U.S. nationals or the national security (national defense, foreign relations, or the economic interests) of the United States.

U.S. GOVERNMENT DESIGNATED FOREIGN TERRORIST ORGANIZATIONS

1. Abu Nidal Organization (ANO)
2. Abu Sayyaf Group (ASG)

3. Al-Aqsa Martyrs Brigade (AAMB)
4. Al-Shabaab (AS)
5. Ansar al-Islam
6. Armed Islamic Group (GIA)
7. Asbat al-Ansar
8. Aum Shinrikyo (AUM)
9. Basque Fatherland and Liberty (ETA)
10. Communist Party of Philippines/New People's Army (CPP/NPA)
11. Continuity Irish Republican Army (CIRA)
12. Gama'a al-Islamiyya (IG)
13. HAMAS
14. Harakat ul-Jihad-i-Islami/Bangladesh (HUJI-B)
15. Harakat ul-Mujahideen (HUM)
16. Hizballah
17. Islamic Jihad Union (IJU)
18. Islamic Movement of Uzbekistan (IMU)
19. Jaish-e-Mohammed (JEM)
20. Jemaah Islamiya (JI)
21. Kahane Chai
22. Kata'ib Hizballah (KH)
23. Kurdistan Workers' Party (PKK)
24. Lashkar e-Tayyiba (LT)
25. Lashkar i Jhangvi (LJ)
26. Liberation Tigers of Tamil Eelam (LTTE)
27. Libyan Islamic Fighting Group (LIFG)
28. Moroccan Islamic Combatant Group (GICM)
29. Mujahadin-e Khalq Organization (MEK)
30. National Liberation Army (ELN)
31. Palestine Liberation Front – Abu Abbas Faction (PLF)
33. Palestinian Islamic Jihad – Shaqaqi Faction (PIJ)
34. Popular Front for the Liberation of Palestine (PFLP)
35. Popular Front for the Liberation of Palestine-General Command (PFLP-GC)
36. Al-Qa'ida (AQ)
37. Al-Qa'ida in Iraq (AQI)
38. Al-Qa'ida in the Islamic Maghreb (AQIM)

39. Real IRA (RIRA)
40. Revolutionary Armed Forces of Colombia (FARC)
41. Revolutionary Organization 17 November (17N)
42. Revolutionary People's Liberation Party/Front (DHKP/C)
43. Revolutionary Struggle (RS)
44. Shining Path (SL)
45. United Self-Defense Forces of Colombia (AUC)

> NOTE: For descriptions of these foreign terrorist organizations,
> please refer to "Country Reports on terrorism 2009" accessible at
> http://www.state.gov/s/ct/rls/crt/2009/140900.htm.

APPENDIX B

Recommended Reading

Noam Chomsky, *Culture of Terrorism* (South End Press, 1988).

Noam Chomsky, *Media Control: The Spectacular Achievements of Propaganda*, 2nd edition (Seven Stories Press, 2002).

Noam Chomsky, *Necessary Illusions* (South End Press, 1989).

Noam Chomsky, *Pirates and Emperors, Old and New* (South End Press, 2003).

Noam Chomsky, *Power and Terror*, expanded edition (Paradigm, 2011).

Noam Chomsky, *Profit Over People: Neoliberalism and Global Order* (Seven Stories Press, 1998).

Noam Chomsky, *Hegemony or Survival* (Metropolitan, 2004).

Noam Chomsky, *Failed States* (Metropolitan, 2007).

Chomsky and Edward S. Herman, *Political Economy of Human Rights* (South End Press, 1979).

Chomsky and Gilbert Achcar, edited by Stephen R. Shalom, *Perilous Power: The Middle East and U.S. Foreign Policy: Dialogues on Terror, Democracy, War, and Justice* (Paradigm, 2006).

John Cooley, *Unholy Wars: Afghanistan, America and International Terrorism* (Pluto, 1999, 2001).

Alex George, ed., *Western State Terrorism* (Polity-Blackwell, 1991).

Fawaz A. Gerges, *The Far Enemy: Why Jihad Went Global* (Cambridge, 2005, 2009).

Fawaz Gerges, *Journey of the Jihadist: Inside Muslim Militancy* (Harcourt, 2006).

Herman, *Real Terror Network* (South End Press, 1982).

Herman and Chomsky, *Manufacturing Consent* (Pantheon, 1998, 2001).

Herman and Gerry O'Sullivan, *The 'Terrorism' Industry* (Pantheon, 1990).

Walter Laqueur, *Age of Terrorism* (Little, Brown and Co., 1987).

Michael McClintock, *Instruments of Statecraft* (Pantheon, 1992).

Project Censored et al., *Censored 2011* (Seven Stories Press, 2010).

Nir Rosen, *Aftermath: Following the Bloodshed of America's Wars in the Muslim World* (Nation Books, 2010)

Paul Wilkinson, *Terrorism and the Liberal State* (NYU Press, 1986).

ABOUT THE AUTHOR

NOAM CHOMSKY was born in Philadelphia, Pennsylvania, on December 7, 1928. He studied linguistics, mathematics, and philosophy at the University of Pennsylvania. In 1955, he received his Ph.D. from the University of Pennsylvania and began teaching at the Massachusetts Institute of Technology, where he is Institute Professor Emeritus in the Department of Linguistics and Philosophy.

During the years 1951 to 1955, Chomsky was a Junior Fellow of the Harvard University Society of Fellows. While a Junior Fellow he completed his doctoral dissertation entitled, "Transformational Analysis." The major theoretical viewpoints of the dissertation appeared in the monograph *Syntactic Structure*, which was published in 1957 and is widely credited with having revolutionized the field of modern linguistics. This formed part of a more extensive work, *The Logical Structure of Linguistic Theory*, circulated in mimeograph in 1955. Most of a 1956 version was published in 1975.

In 1961, Chomsky was appointed full professor in the Department of Modern Languages and Linguistics (now the Department of Linguistics and Philosophy) at MIT. From 1966 to 1976 he held the Ferrari P. Ward Professorship of Modern Languages and Linguistics. In 1976 he was appointed Institute Professor, a position he held until 2002.

Chomsky is the author of numerous influential political works, including *Hopes and Prospects* (Haymarket Books) *Interventions* (City Lights/Open Media Series), *Failed States* (Metropolitan Books), *Hegemony or Survival: Amer-*

ica's Quest for Global Dominance (Metropolitan Books), *Media Control* (Seven Stories Press/Open Media Series), *Manufacturing Consent: The Political Economy of the Mass Media* with Ed Herman (Pantheon), *Necessary Illusions* (South End Press), *Understanding Power* (New Press), and many other titles.

In 1988, Chomsky received the Kyoto Prize in Basic Science, given "to honor those who have contributed significantly to the scientific, cultural, and spiritual development of mankind." The prize noted that "Dr. Chomsky's theoretical system remains an outstanding monument of 20th century science and thought. He can certainly be said to be one of the great academicians and scientists of this century." On June 1, 2011, Noam Chomsky was named 2011 winner of the Sydney Peace Prize.

Chomsky lives in Lexington, Massachusetts.

ABOUT OPEN MEDIA

OPEN MEDIA is a movement-oriented publishing project committed to the vision of "one world in which many worlds fit"—a world with social justice, democracy, and human rights for all people. Founded during wartime in 1991 by Greg Ruggiero, Open Media has a history of producing critically acclaimed and best-selling titles that address the most urgent political and social issues of our time.

ABOUT SEVEN STORIES PRESS

SEVEN STORIES PRESS is an independent book publisher based in New York City. We publish works of the imagination by such writers as Nelson Algren, Russell Banks, Octavia E. Butler, Ani DiFranco, Assia Djebar, Ariel Dorfman, Coco Fusco, Barry Gifford, Lee Stringer, and Kurt Vonnegut, to name a few, together with political titles by voices of conscience, including the Boston Women's Health Collective, Noam Chomsky, Angela Y. Davis, Human Rights Watch, Derrick Jensen, Ralph Nader, Gary Null, Project Censored, Barbara Seaman, Gary Webb, and Howard Zinn, among many others. Seven Stories Press believes publishers have a special responsibility to defend free speech and human rights, and to celebrate the gifts of the human imagination, wherever we can. For additional information, visit www.sevenstories.com.

In *9-11*, published in November 2001 and arguably the single most influential post-9-11 book, internationally renowned thinker Noam Chomsky bridged the information gap around the World Trade Center attacks, cutting through the tangle of political opportunism, expedient patriotism, and general conformity that choked off American discourse in the months immediately following. Chomsky placed the attacks in context, marshaling his deep and nuanced knowledge of American foreign policy to trace the history of American political aggression—in the Middle East and throughout Latin America as well as in Indonesia, in Afghanistan, in India and Pakistan—at the same time warning against America's increasing reliance on military rhetoric and violence in its response to the attacks, and making the critical point that the mainstream media and public intellectuals were failing to make: any escalation of violence as a response to violence will inevitably lead to further, and bloodier, attacks on innocents in America and around the world.

This new edition of *9-11*, published on the tenth anniversary of the attacks and featuring *Was There an Alternative?*, a new text by Chomsky, reminds us that today, just as much as ten years ago, information and clarity remain our most valuable tools in the struggle to prevent future violence against the innocent, both at home and abroad.